Making Classic Carved Furniture:

The Queen Anne Stool

Ron Clarkson
&
Tom Heller

Text written with
and photography
Douglas Congdon-Martin

Schiffer Publishing Ltd
77 Lower Valley Road, Atglen, PA 19310

Acknowledgements

We wish to thank Jody Garrett and all of the people at Woodcraft Supply Corporation for their valuable assistance in this project. James Guthrie for letting us photograph the chair we built for him, for use in the gallery.

Also, we thank Peter Schiffer and all of the fine people at Schiffer Publishing, Ltd., especially Douglas Congdon-Martin for his patience and understanding and his invaluable insight, without which this project would have never been completed.

Published by Schiffer Publishing, Ltd.
77 Lower Valley Road
Atglen, PA 19310
Please write for a free catalog.
This book may be purchased from the publisher.
Please include $2.95 postage.
Try your bookstore first.

We are interested in hearing from authors
with book ideas on related subjects.

Library of Congress Catalog Number: 93-87051

Printed in the United States of America.
ISBN: 0-88740-588-6

DESIGNED BY MARK S. BALBACH

Contents

Introduction

Beginning with our prehistoric ancestors, we have had a need to decorate our surroundings. Whether it be crude drawings on cave walls or fine arts and paintings, human beings have taken their view of nature and enhanced their lives. Over time, they acquired the knowledge and skills to put life into their art: dimension. Looking at everyday things, flowers, trees, animals, they transformed mundane utilitarian objects into things of beauty. One of the ways to this transformation was with carving.

Our purpose in writing this book is to provide the individual who enjoys creating his own pieces of furniture with the information he or she needs. The step-by-step process we outline will enhance the furniture makers endeavors, turning them into beautiful as well as useful items.

In selecting the piece shown in this book, we hope to demonstrate the techniques needed, without getting too complicated. The foot stool meets the purpose. The same techniques and the same elements, however, can be transferred to other projects as well, including chairs, tables, and other pieces.

Before one begins, there are a few fundamental things that are necessary if you are to achieve good results. First, if drawing is not second nature to you, a complete set of plans and full-sized renderings are displayed in the book. However, the need for fundamental drawing techniques are inherently important in the art of carving. We would recommend getting a good book on beginning drawing or taking an adult education course to help improve your skills.

Second, you will need good quality carving tools. This doesn't mean you have to get a second mortgage on your home! Just be sure your tools will handle the job you've set for them and make sure to keep them sharp. A complete listing of tools used for this project can be found in the book. If you do not have the exact tool we used, a close substitute will be fine.

Third, and probably most important of all, is PATIENCE. Remember, you are creating an object of beauty, something you can be proud of for a lifetime.

We chose mahogany as our wood for this project because of its even grain properties, but any good wood can be used.

If you follow our book carefully, you will be able to reproduce this standard 18th century piece of American furniture.

We hope you enjoy our endeavor and find woodworking of this caliber to be fun and satisfying, ending with a project well done.

Dedication

To my family, for their continued support, enabling me to realize my dreams.

Tom Heller

To Ida, simply the best.

Ron Clarkson

CONSTRUCTION DETAIL

MORTICE & TENON

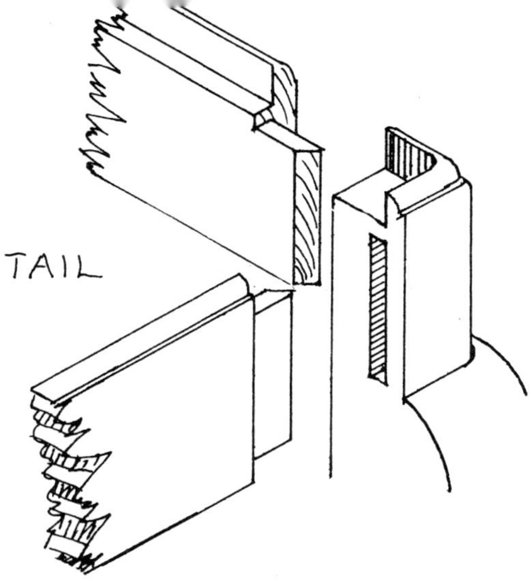

FRONT & SIDE RAILS DETAIL

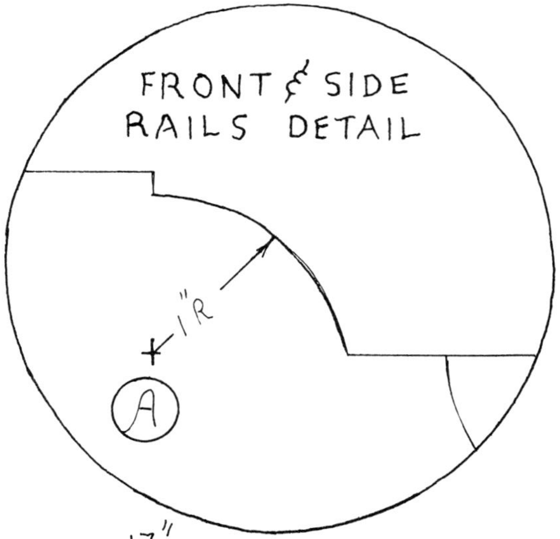

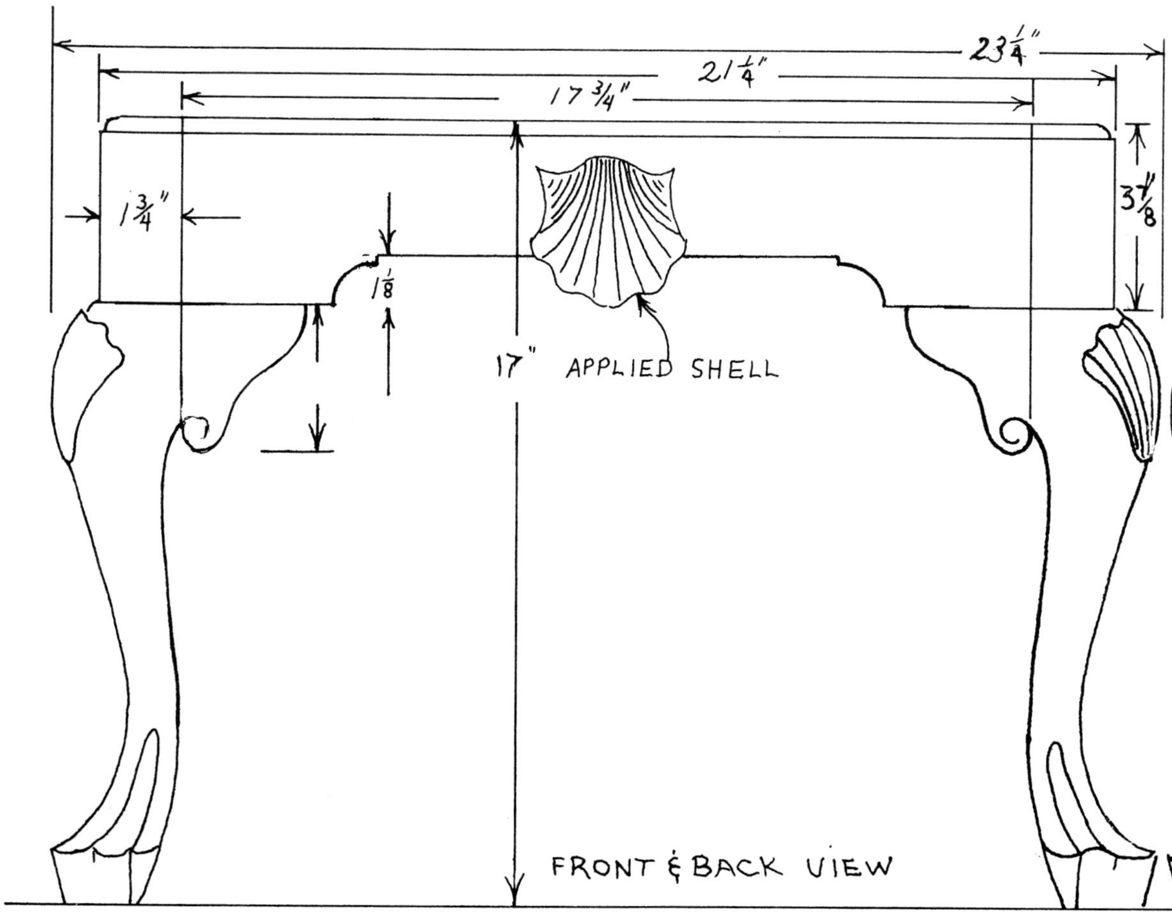

FRONT & BACK VIEW

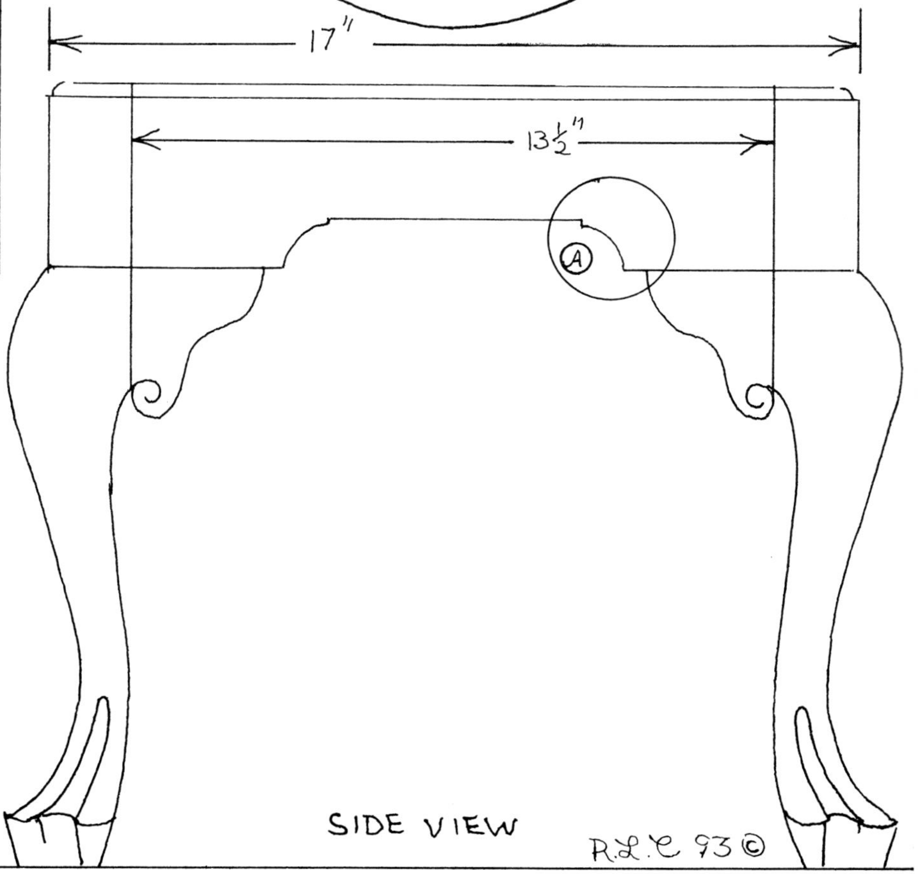

SIDE VIEW

R.L.C. 93 ©

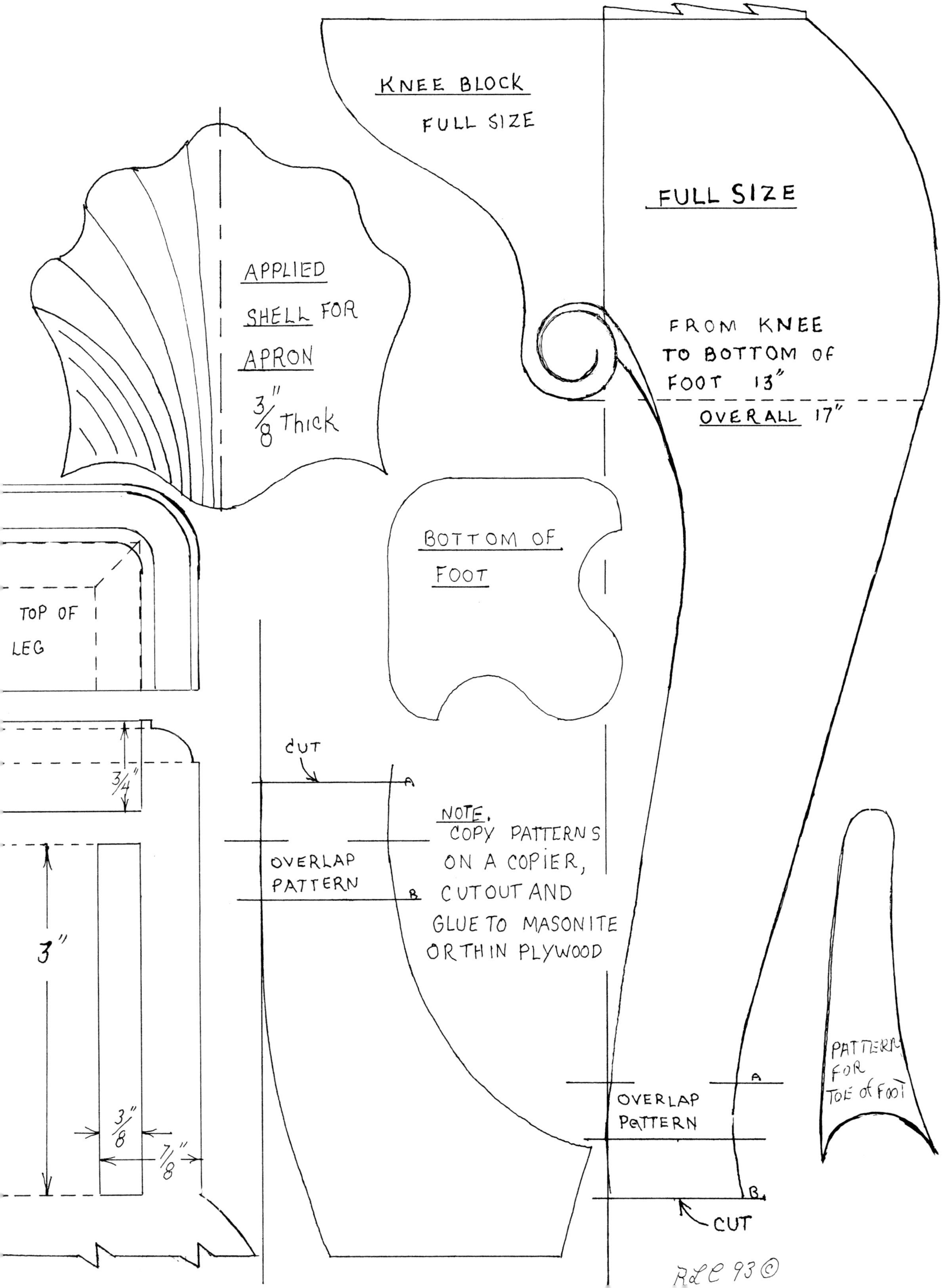
KNEE BLOCK
FULL SIZE
FULL SIZE
APPLIED SHELL FOR APRON
3/8" Thick
FROM KNEE TO BOTTOM OF FOOT 13"
OVERALL 17"
BOTTOM OF FOOT
TOP OF LEG
3/4"
3"
3/8"
7/8"
CUT
A
OVERLAP PATTERN
B
NOTE.
COPY PATTERNS ON A COPIER, CUTOUT AND GLUE TO MASONITE OR THIN PLYWOOD
PATTERN FOR TOE of FOOT
A
OVERLAP PATTERN
B
CUT
RLC 93©

the Stool

The block we will use for the leg is a 2 7/8" square block that is 17" long. The wood is Honduras mahogany. If this is unavailable, walnut or cherry could be substituted. The mahogany, however, is an excellent carving wood and is readily available.

When selecting your wood, a straight and even grain is best for carving purposes. The density of the wood is also a consideration. The denser, heavier the wood, the tighter and smoother the grain, giving you nice, crisp carvings. The softer the wood the more difficult the carving and the sharper your tools need to be.

Cut a template from 1/4" or 1/8" masonite or plywood. The measured drawing is in the front of the book.

Mark the mortises with a mortising gauge, and cut them out before laying the pattern. The notch at the top corner of the leg is to hold the seat. Normally we would not cut this out until much later, but for the purposes of the book it was easier to do it ahead of time.

To cut out the legs on the bandsaw, you need to stop the cut before a piece is totally separated so the pattern will stay intact. This enables you to cut on both surfaces. We suggest you practice on scrap lumber, before using good (and expensive!) wood. The cut should be outside the pattern line, leaving you plenty of wood to work with. The first cut begins at the end of the post and makes the turn down the knee.

The leg pattern is laid on the outside surfaces of the leg, so the knees meet at the corner.

Stop before coming out of the wood. This leaves the pattern on the other side future use.

The second cut starts at the toe and goes up to the knee.

Cut the heel, leaving it attached.

Again, stop before the blade emerges from the wood.

Finally, do the same on the underside of the toe.

Cut out behind the knee in the same way, not going far enough to make the piece fall out.

The first side cut. As you can see, all the pieces are still attached by a small stretch of wood.

Turn the piece so the uncut pattern is up, and, beginning at the post, cut the front edge of the leg. This can be done in one continuous cut.

and the heel...

The pieces should fall away as this cut continues.

and toe.

Continue behind the knee...

Go back and finish the cuts...

from the first side.

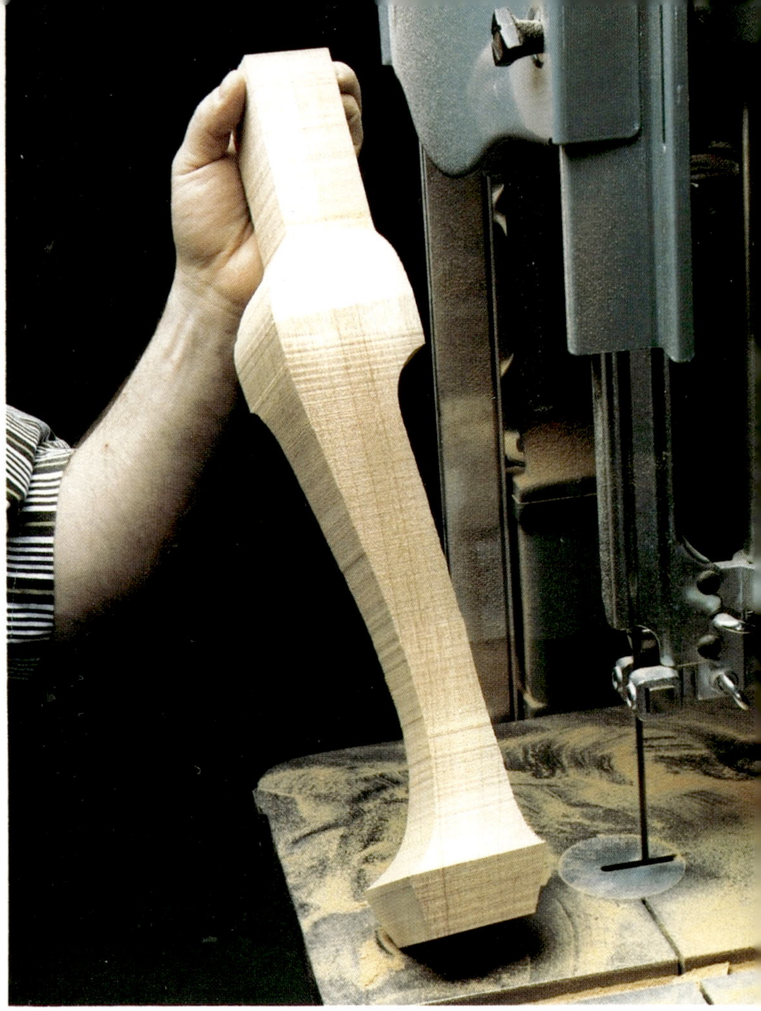

The result

This Easy Carv'n Vise is perfect for holding the leg for carving.

If that vise is not available, something like this will work. This holding jig can be easily made at home from two pieces of two-by-four, an all-thread, and some nuts. It is held in a bench vise. You will see it in use later in the book.

Some carvers draw "witness marks" to establish symmetry, but we prefer to work without them. The knee really needs to appeal to the eye, so the eye is our main judge of symmetry. We are after a natural, animal-like leg. Begin with the spokeshave to remove as much wood as possible. The knee will have the most removed.

Continue shaving down the ankle.

An alternative way to remove this wood is to use a bench chisel.

Work down from the knee and begin to round off the leg.

Stop about here to leave wood for carving.

With curved leg you will run into a change in grain direction and begin to cut against the grain.

This work should move rather quickly, with nice easy strokes. This is how the eighteenth century craftsperson would have worked, and it gives the piece a spontaneity and individuality that cannot be achieved if every stroke is carefully and slowly measured.

When this happens, switch your shaving direction.

Continue on the other side. To get the ankle round, it is best to take it to octagonal first. Without doing this the tendency is to go to oval, or, more likely, to a square shape with rounded edges.

Once it is to octagonal...

With the back edge shaved, it begins to take shape.

go back and rough round it with the spokeshave.

At the ankle the diameter should be about 1 1/8". You can use a caliper to measure this.

Small, finger spokeshaves are available for some of the tighter turns.

This area at the bottom of the ankle benefits from it.

The rounded side of a rasp may also be used. This pattern maker's rasp has a random pattern to the teeth that gives a smooth effect while removing a nice quantity of wood.

Continue to work your way around the leg. This also takes away the bandsaw marks and begins the smoothing process.

Go back occasionally and check your progress.

With the ankle done, go back and true up the knee. You are trying to create a relatively smooth, even surface for the carving. Remember to leave the top inch or so of the knee untouched.

The end of the rough shaping. The feet are left square for the carving.

Now we move to the rails. The rails are 3 7/8" wide and 7/8" thick. The front and back rails are 17 3/4" long from shoulder to shoulder with an additional 1 1/4" for the tenons at each end giving an overall length of 20 1/4". The side rails are 13 1/2" shoulder to shoulder plus 1 1/4" at each end for the tenons, with an overall length of 16" overall. The tenons must be cut before laying the patterns for the edge. The pattern for the front and back rails is designed to work from the shoulders to the middle. Line it up with the bottom edge and mark from the end to the center.

Turn the pattern around and do the same from the other shoulder.

The result.

Use the same template to mark the side rails, but do not draw the radius for the shell.

The side rail marked.

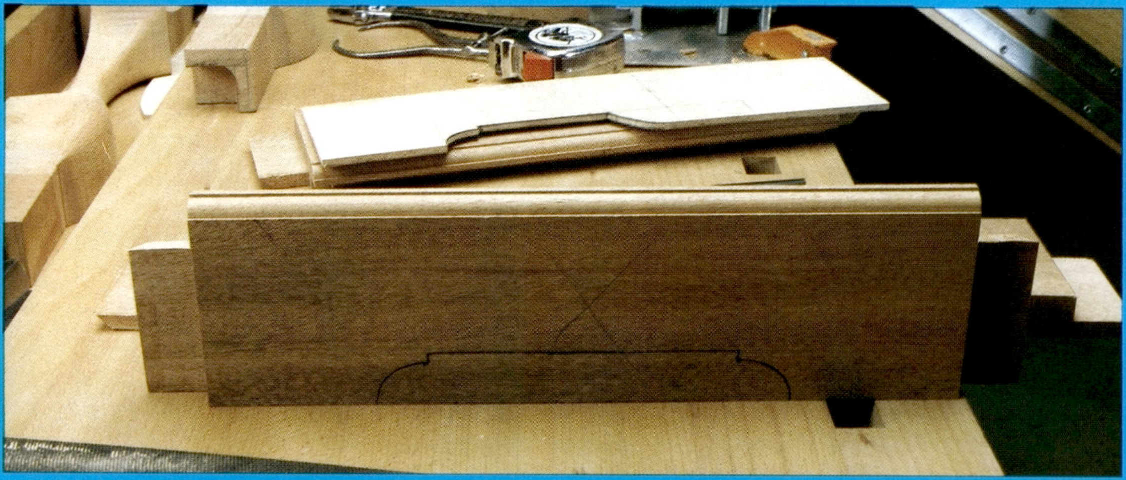

Run an edge along the top with a router or a plane. There are several choices you may make for this edge.

After running the edge cut a rabbit on the opposite edge to hold the slip seat. This can be done on a table saw or with a router. It is 3/4" deep...

and about 7/16" wide, although this may vary.

Test fit the legs. The top of the leg should be even with the top of the rail. Check for squareness by measuring from corner to corner. Place clamps centered at the joint of the leg and apron to be sure the joints are snug. Finally check to be sure the whole stool is level. When everything is set, number the legs and aprons so they will match when reassembled.

The wood for the knee block is 2 7/8" thick x 2 7/16". A seven inch long block will produce the two knee returns for one leg. Hold the block under the apron and against the leg and mark it. Each fitting is custom fitted, so number the leg and the knee block.

Flip to the other end of the block and mark the other knee return.

Lay the pattern so the joining edge comes to the same corner as the line of the knee. Mark it, and repeat for each leg.

Move to the bandsaw again and cut the knee shape. As you did with leg, don't cut all the way through, so the pattern of the profile stays intact.

Turn the piece and cut the profile of the knee return.

Go back and knock off the knee shape.

On the side rails, cut straight into the fillet on each side.

Come back and cut the cavetto...

continuing across to the opposite fillet. Do the other cavetto, and clean its opposing fillet.

In the front and rear rails, make stop cuts on either side of the shell shield...

and in the fillets.

Cut the rest as with side rails.

Reassemble the piece, being sure to match the legs with their mated apron rails.

With the piece assembled we glue the knee returns to the legs. We don't want them to stick to the apron, so we cover the apron with masking tape.

Apply yellow carpenter's glue to the knee return. We apply glue to only one surface, using enough to make it stick. A little glue should ooze out of the joint.

Put the return in place.

Apply a clamp with light pressure. Clean up and leaking glue.

The knee return pushed the apron up a little, so we use a mallet and block to tap it into place.

The clamp set-up on one leg. Repeat on the other three legs.

The pattern for the applied shells is based on a 3 1/4" circle with a scallop design over it. To be sure the pattern is correct, use the gouges you will use to carve it to cut it out. We use a number 8/13 gouge, the 8 referring to the sweep of the chisel and the 13 referring to the width in millimeters. These will vary between manufacturers. Press the gouge into the pattern to cut the convex curves...

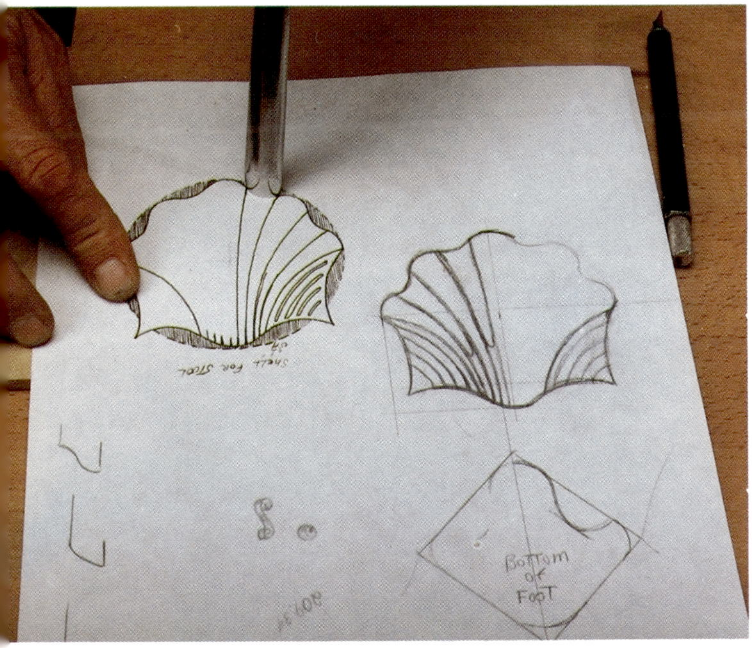

and the concave. If you are creating your own pattern you can use the chisel in the design process as well.

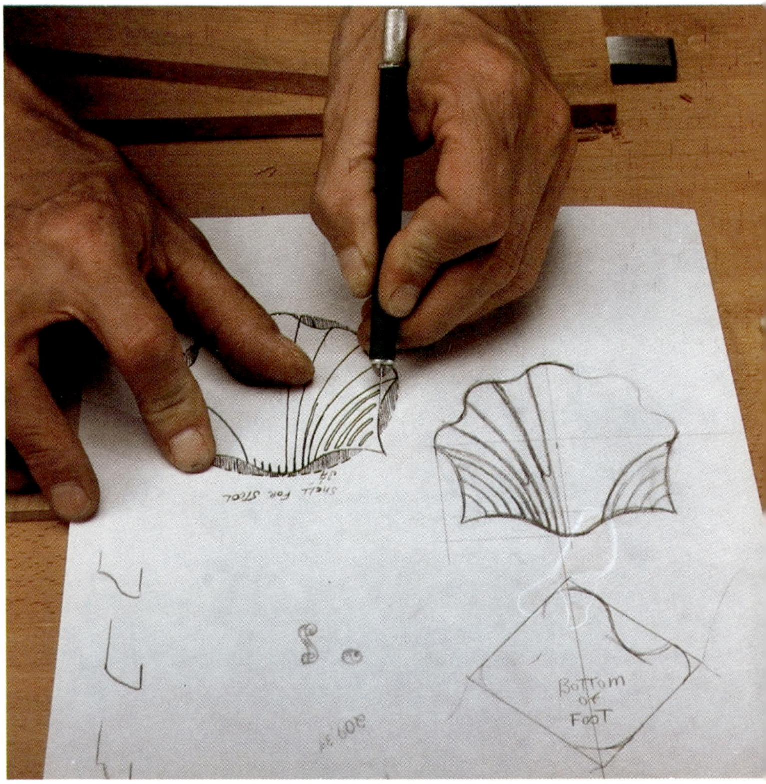

Cut the pattern out. On the scalloped edge you should only need to cut the tabs between the chisel cuts. Any stiff paper or cardboard will work well for the pattern.

Transfer the pattern to a mahogany board planed to a thickness of 3/8" and wide enough to fit the pattern. The grain will run from side to side, the same direction as the apron.

Cut the pattern to "the fat side" of the line with a bandsaw, coping saw, or jig saw.

and secure to the bench. Here I use bench dogs.

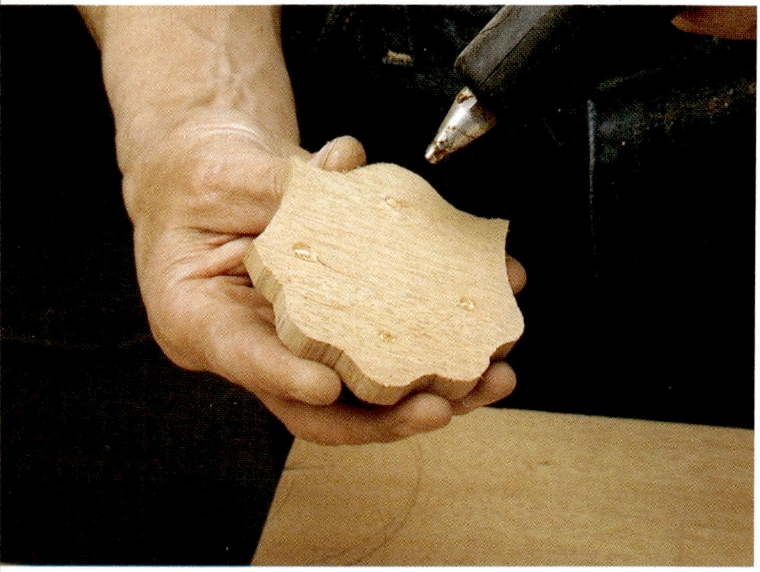

To secure the shell for carving, we apply three or four drops of hot glue to the back. This is enough to hold it, but not enough to prevent us from breaking it apart when the carving is complete.

Start at the top and begin by bevelling the edge.

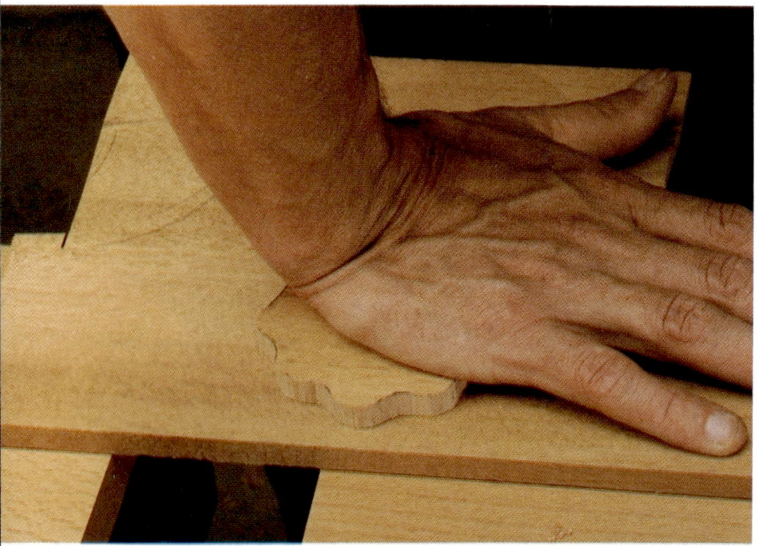

Apply the shell blank to a piece of scrap wood...

Continue around the sides. The object is to make the center of the shell the highest point.

Go across the center of the bottom.

Connect the dots.

We need to transfer the outer rays of the center portion of the shell, by punching holes along the line in the pattern with an awl or other sharp tool. We need this line before we lower the surface of the shell's ears.

This creates a nice easy to follow line.

Set a stop in this line by driving a fairly flat gouge into it. Don't go too deep or you will split the wood.

Trim the ear along the stop with a chisel.

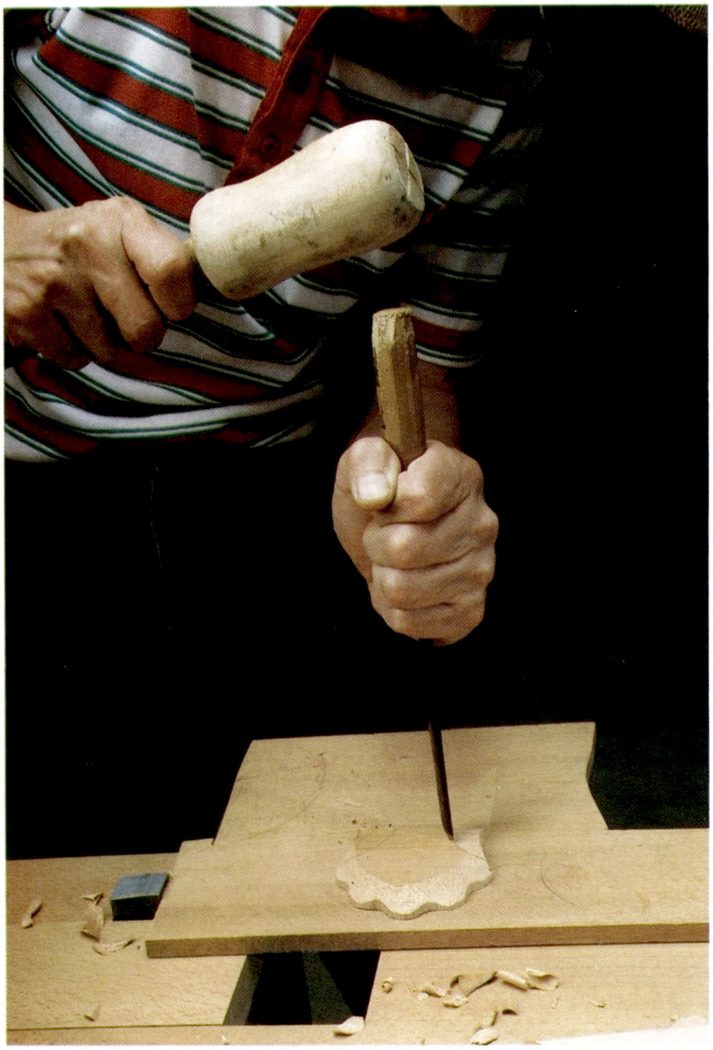

Repeat the process...

until you've brought the ear down to thickness of about 1/8".

After the stop has been well established, things can be speeded up by deepening the stop using a bent v-gouge.

You want to bring it down to about this point. Repeat the process on the other ear.

Progress. We can now finish rounding it up.

Begin by rounding the curved edges of the central shell, where it meets the ears.

Do the same on each side.

Basically I'm moving from the edges toward the center. I use a combination of sight and touch to keep things even. I also move around from place to place to avoid cutting too long in one place.

At times it is necessary to go across the grain, and if you have a sharp chisel, this shouldn't present any problem.

When you get to this point you can use a wide sweep gouge to make the curve nice and even. Use it with the cup side against the work.

At other places it may work best to go diagonally across the grain in a skewing action.

Refer to the pattern and draw in the rays of the shell. We like to do it by eye, but if you are more comfortable you can use dividers to mark them.

Draw one side first and mark the areas to be gouged for the concave cuts.

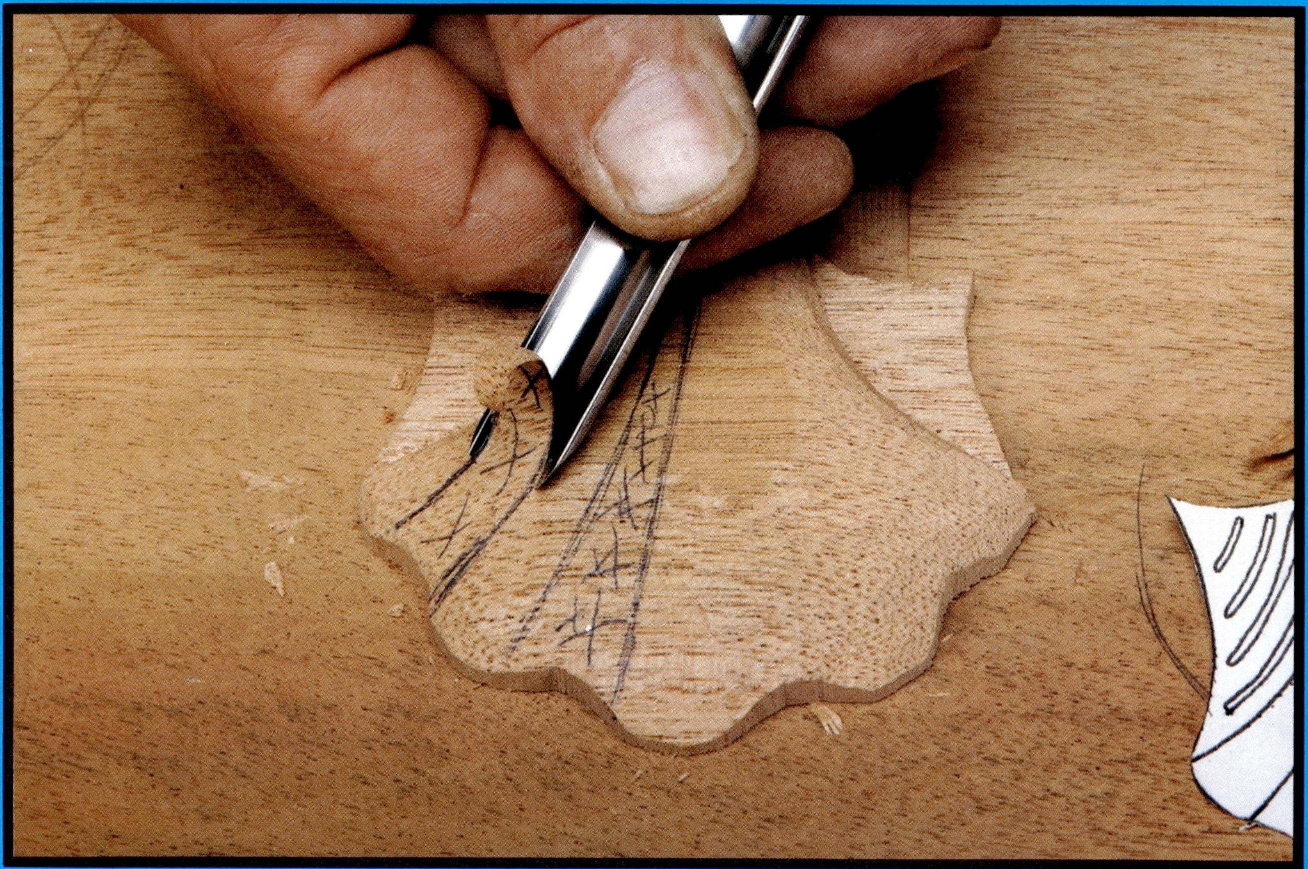

Remove the marked areas with a gouge. Begin at the base of the shell and work your way to the wider, deeper part.

When you get to the end push the gouge in at a slight angle to clean up the cut.

Make the cut in the same way.

The result.

Go back to the original gouge to trim the end.

I was getting some tear in my first cut so I'm switching to a gouge that is deeper and has more sweep.

To keep an edge on my tools I hone them on a piece of split cowhide impregnated with rouges. The red rouge is finer...

Pull the gouge through the emery compound, starting on one edge...

than the black emery compound.

turning the blade as you pull...

and ending up on the other edge.

Repeat with the finer red rouge.

Fold the leather and pull the cup of the gouge across the fold.

The honing process may create a slight burr on the edge of the gouge. This can be removed by driving the gouge into a piece of wood...

and giving it a turn.

Draw in the remaining rays of the shell to match the other side.

Shade the area that will be gouged out.

As before, with your gouge begin to cut at the narrow base of the shell and work your way to the deeper wider top.

Use a gouge with less of a sweep as you approach the end of the cut to get the taper you need.

With the same gouge, cut straight down at the end of the cut to clean it up.

To shape the convex ridges of the shell I use a back bent gouge. It curve is opposite of the regular gouge. The alternative would be to use a flat chisel with the beveled edge against the work, or a combination of both.

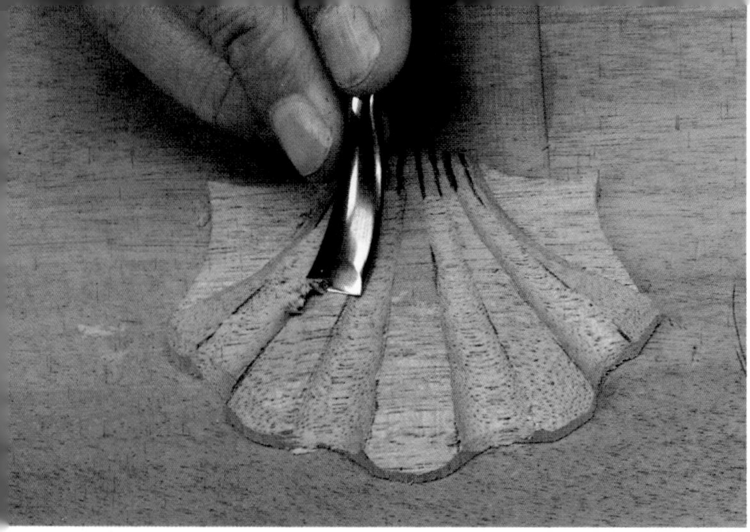

Work along one edge of the ridge at a time. You will have some complicated grain situations with this phase of the carving. On one side of the ridge, you are cutting through the grain at a skewed angle, which is fairly easy and safe.

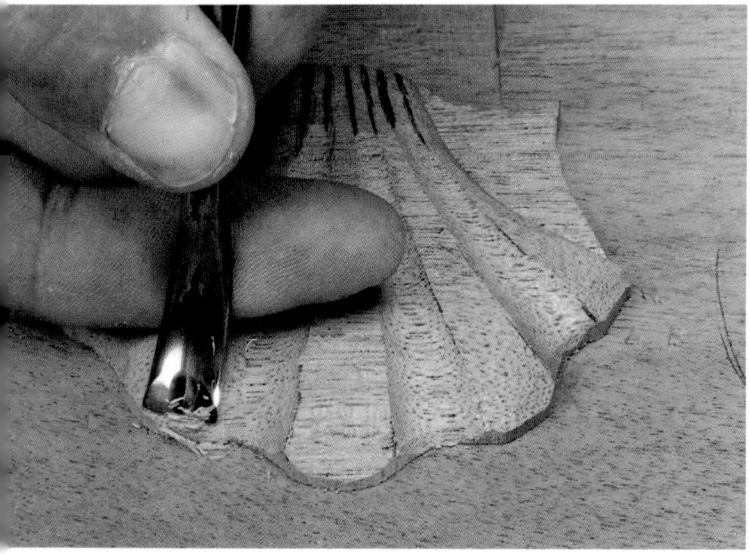

On the other side, however, you are cutting at an angle that goes into the grain. You don't want to turn the piece, because you will be cutting up hill and will end up going into grain anyway. That leaves two ways to approach this problem. The first is to work from the end back to the heel of the shell. Take small bites...

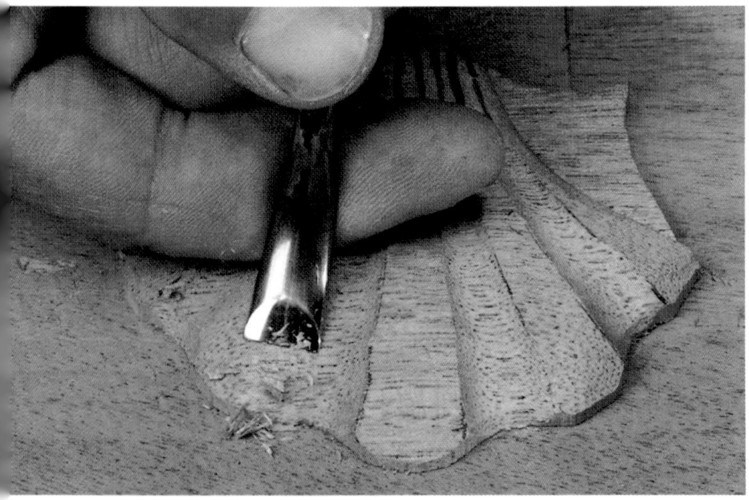

and work your way...

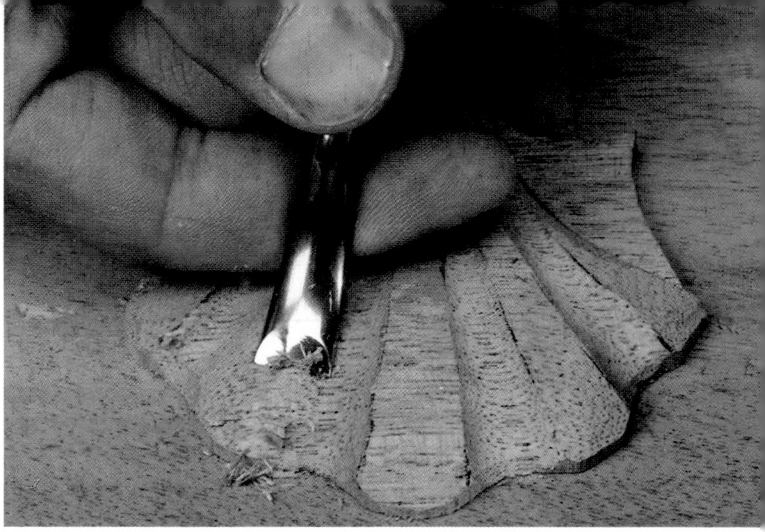

back. This method works because it takes small bites and eliminates the possibility of tearing.

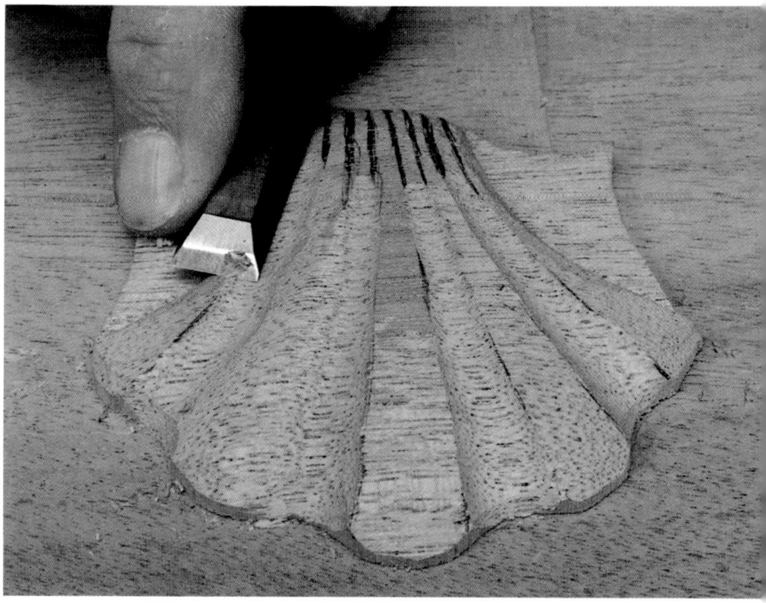

The other method is to use very, very sharp flat chisel with the bevel up and the flat surface against the wood. By cutting on a skewed angle, you can start at the heel...

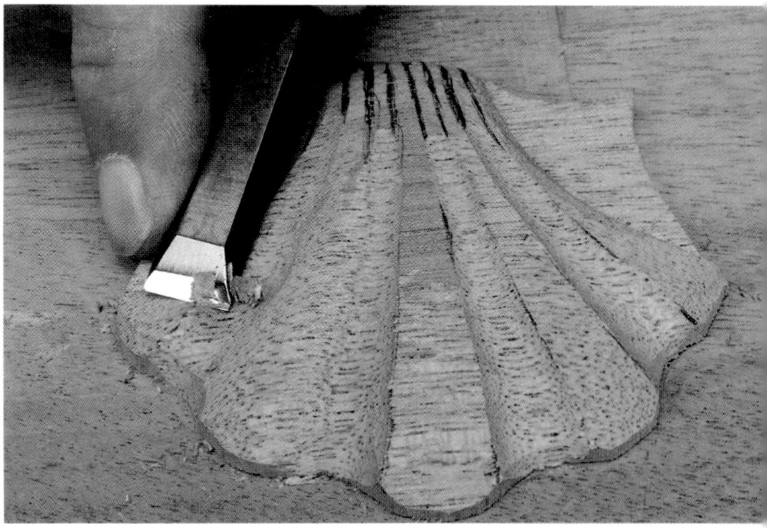

and work your way to the end. If you are tearing the wood, stop and hone your chisel to an even finer edge.

Continue to round all the ridges of the shell.

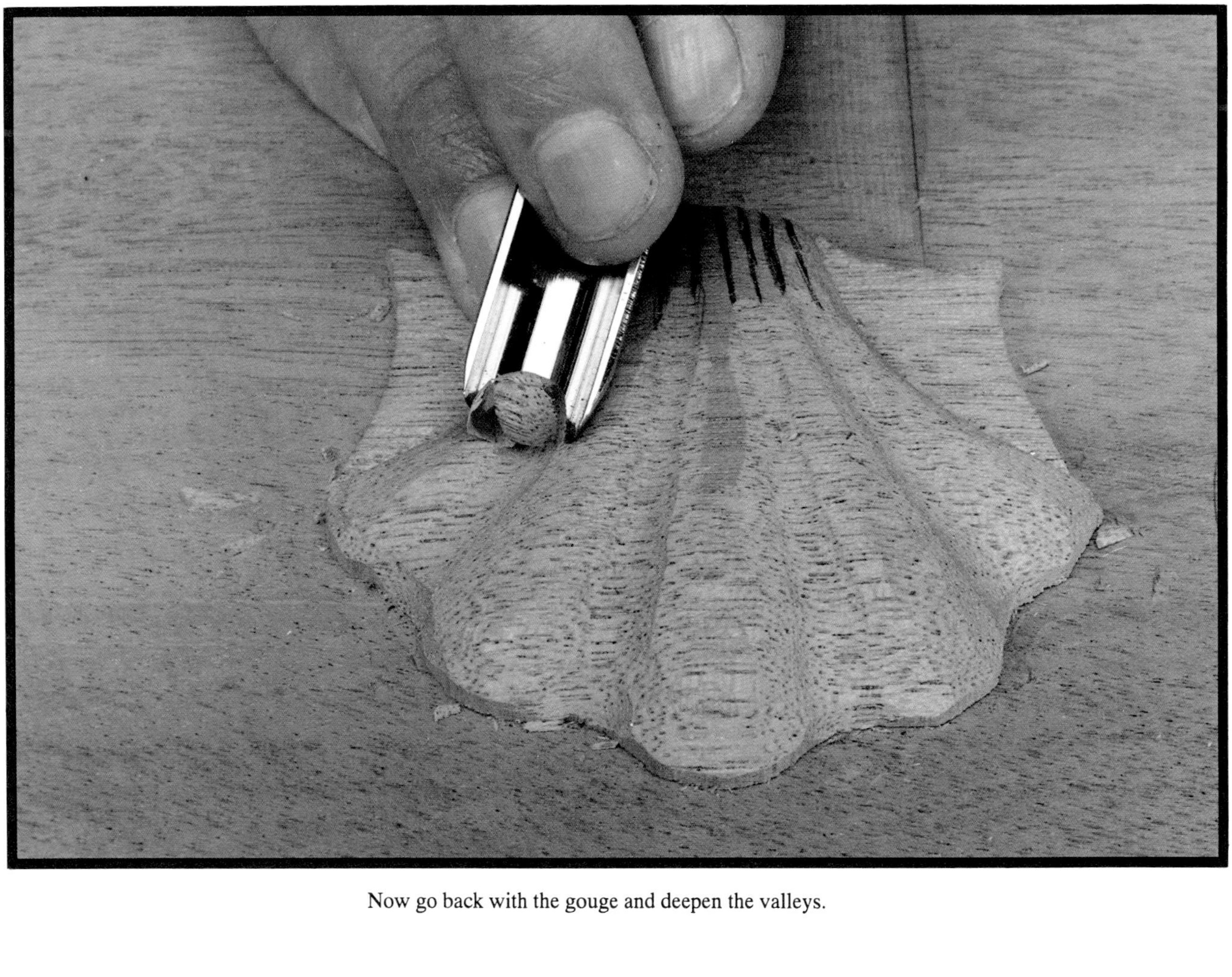

Now go back with the gouge and deepen the valleys.

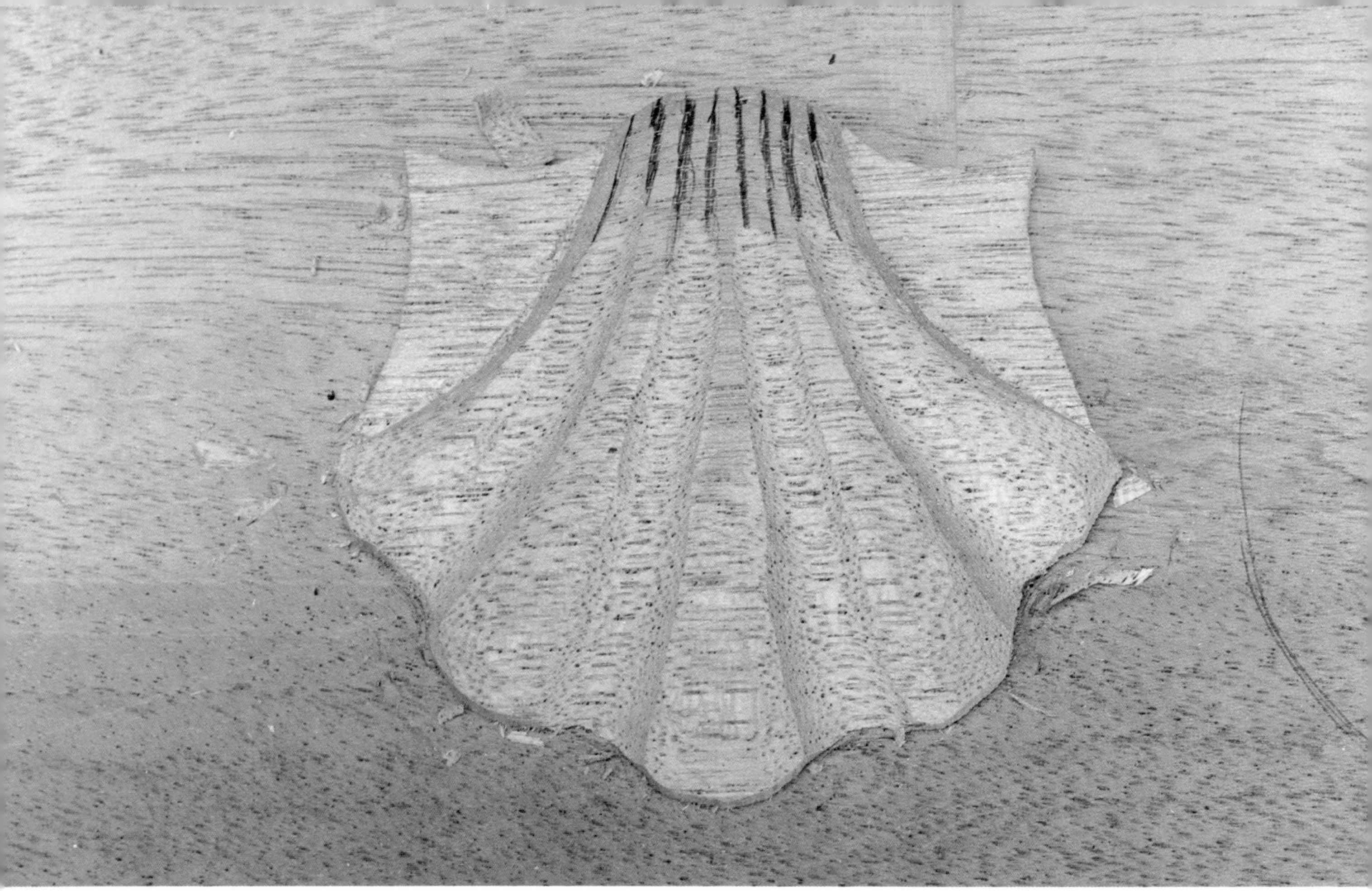

The goal is a nice even taper that goes almost to the final depth, like the one on the left. The importance of sharp tools cannot be overstated. Without them these carvings are almost impossible. Continue with the other valleys in the same way. As you can see, the deeper we go the more definition the shell has. The thickness of the shell at the ends of the valleys is about 1/8".

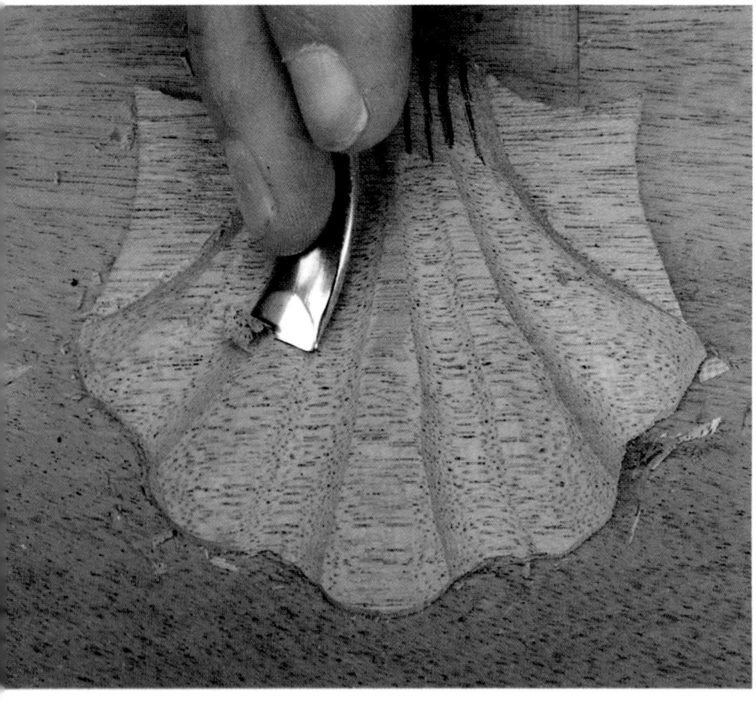

Go back and round over the ridges.

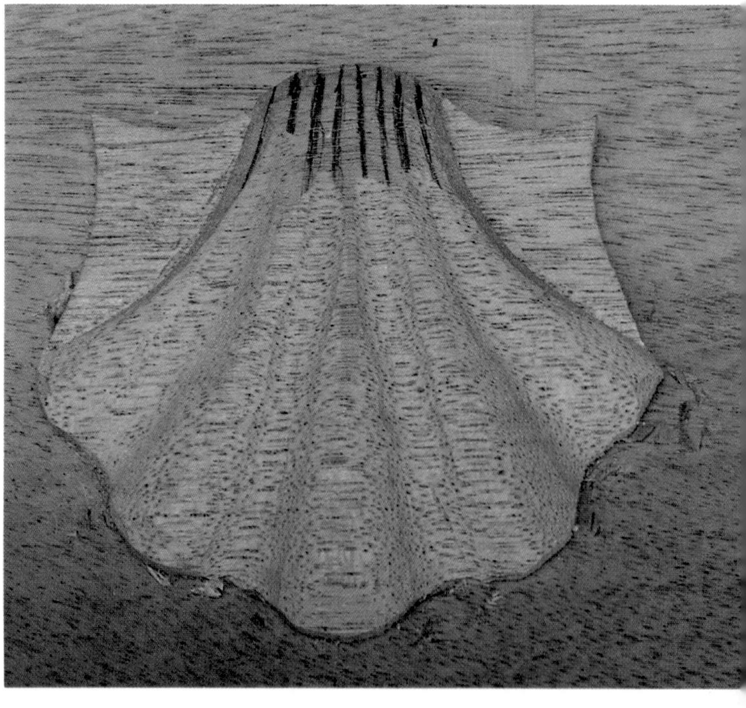

Progress.

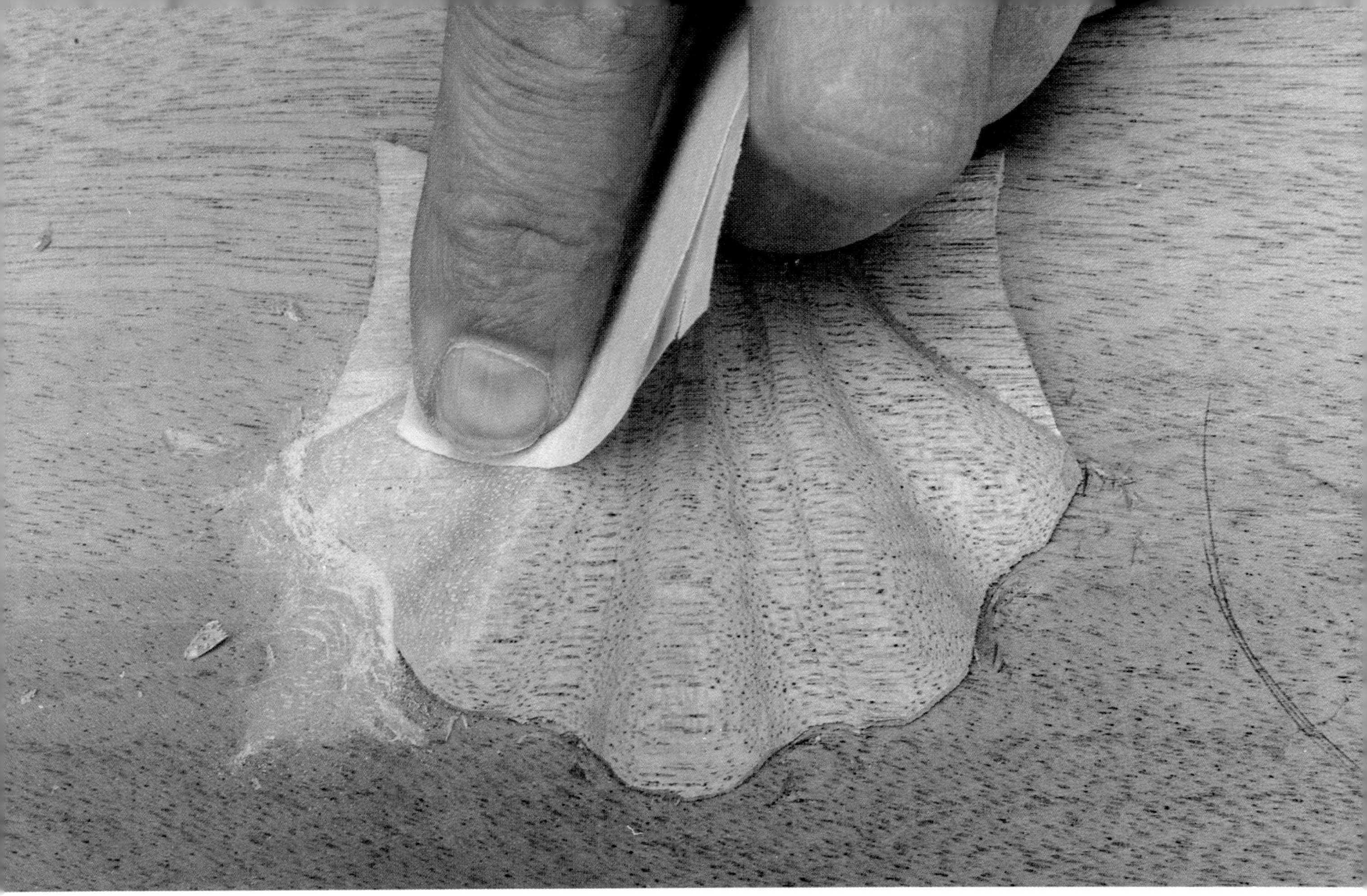

Some carvers would cringe at my next step, because sanding leaves abrasives on the wood that can harm chisels. But I like to smooth things up at this point. I need to redraw my lines and the sanding gives me a better surface to draw on. It also gives me a sense of whether my contours are correct. I use 180 grit sandpaper, which brings the piece to an almost finished smoothness.

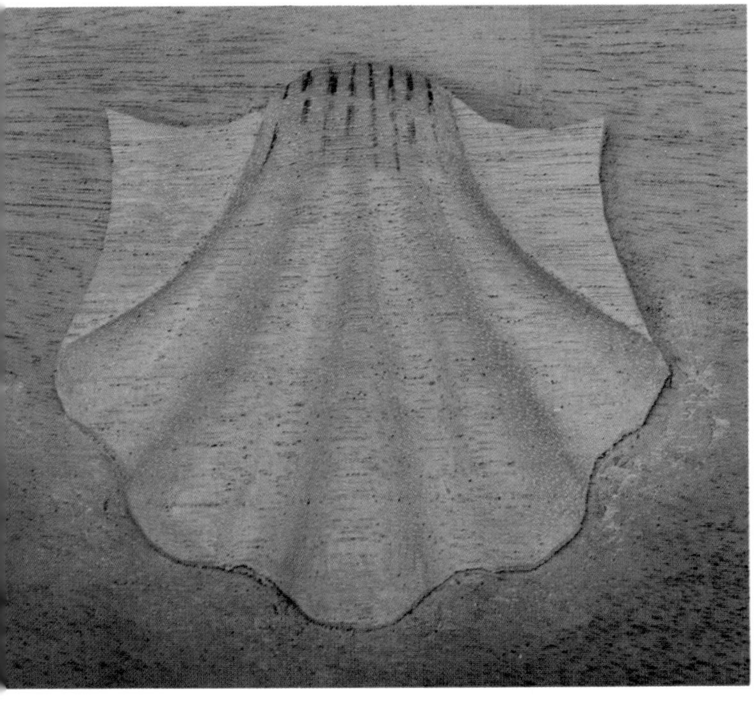

With the sanding done...

I switch to a Scotchbrite™ pad in a very fine grit. This abrasive pad does not leave any abrasives, and in fact helps remove the particles left by the sandpaper.

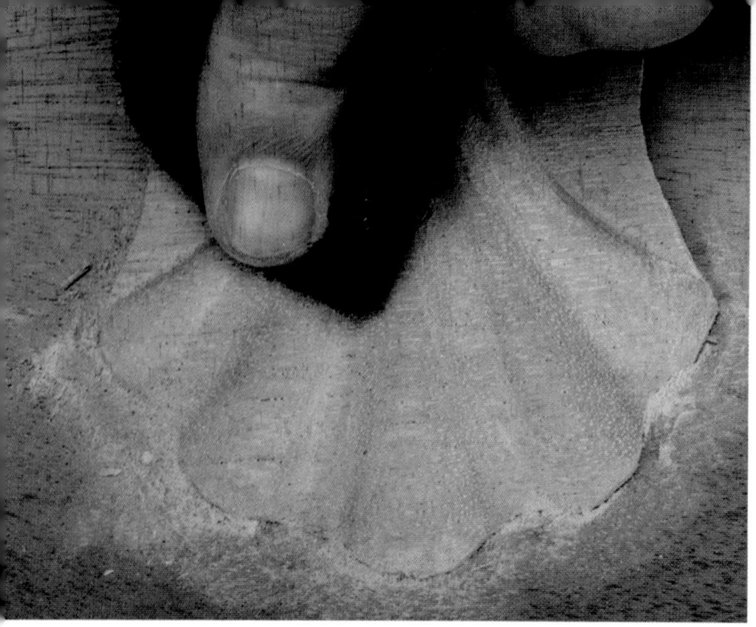

It leaves a very smooth, almost polished surface. There are nine segments to the main section of the shell. At the bottom they are marked at equal widths. The next step is to divide the top and redraw the rays.

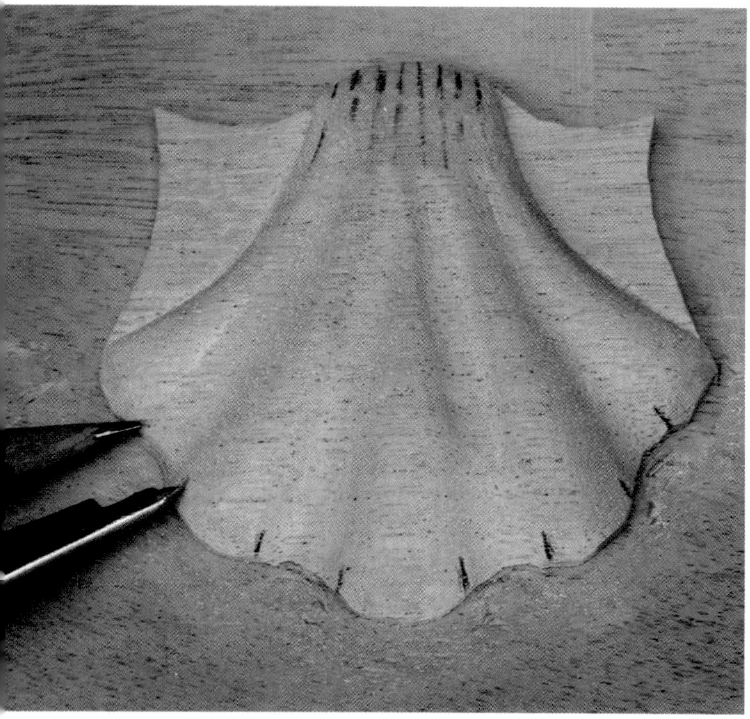

The valleys at the top will all be equal width, while the ridges will vary. The outside ridges will be equal and the narrowest. The next set will also be equal and a little wider than the outside. The middle ridge will be the widest. this is done pretty much by eye. Begin by using a scribe to determine a good width for the valleys. Transfer this width to each valley. This will establish the width of the ridges as well.

Draw the lines freehand from the heel to the top. We're a little more careful with these lines because unlike the first set, these will be permanently carved into the piece.

The lines drawn. This really must be done by eye. It serves the carver well to develop drawing skills and a good eye.

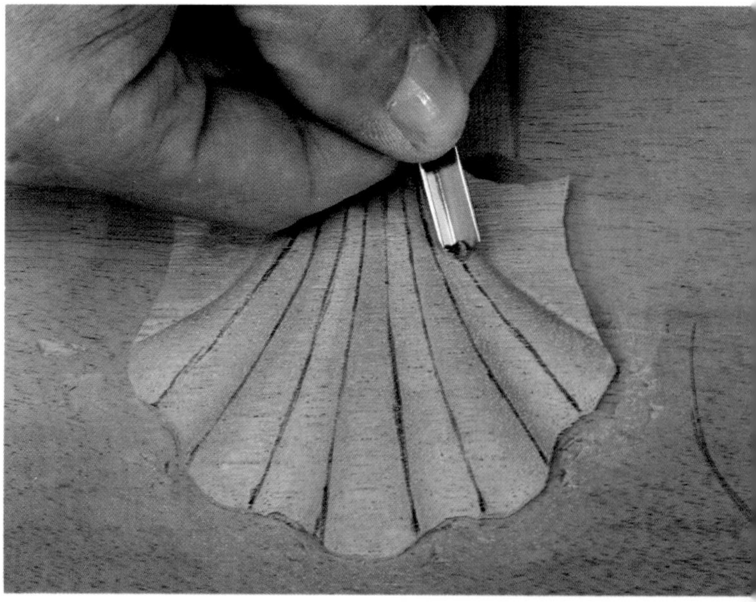

Beginning about 3/4" inch from the heel, follow the lines with a v-tool. During the first part of the cut, the "V" is pretty much straight up and down.

As you move toward the end, the tool leans toward the ridge and away from the valley. You want to do these lines with one long smooth cut.

At the end of the line cut straight down.

Continue with the other lines.

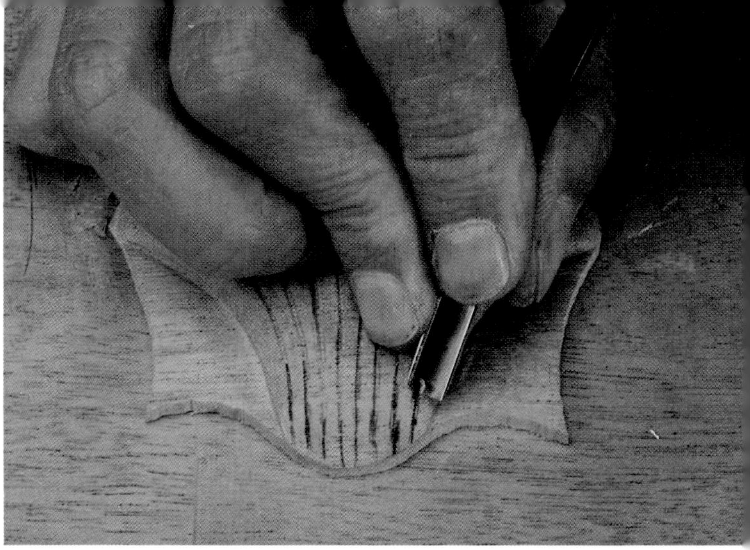

Now turn the piece around and finish the lines at the heel.

Progress.

Round the ridges back to the lines created by the v-tool. Use extra care here so you don't chip or tear the wood.

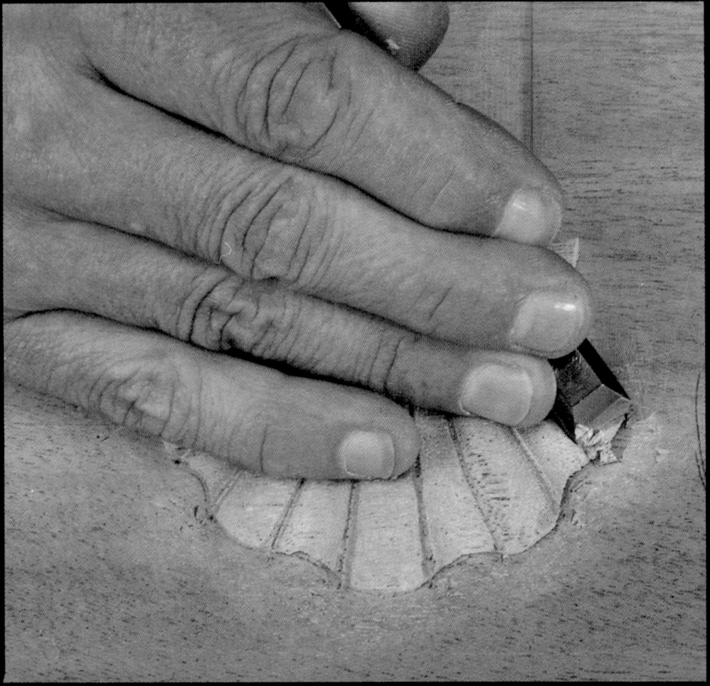

Again, when working against the grain, it is helpful to work backwards from the end. This relieves resistance in the wood and helps prevent tearing.

Follow the lines with a small (11/1) veiner. Try to use one continuous cut for each line.

Draw the lines in the ears of the shell. These start in about 1/16" from the edges of the ears, and follow the sweep of the central part of the shell. We use four on each ear.

The carving is complete.

To pry the carving from the cutting board, use a wide chisel and go with the grain, first from one side...

Situate the shell so the bottom corner of the first ridge is aligned with the straight edge of the rail.

then the other.

Trace the outline of the shell on the rail.

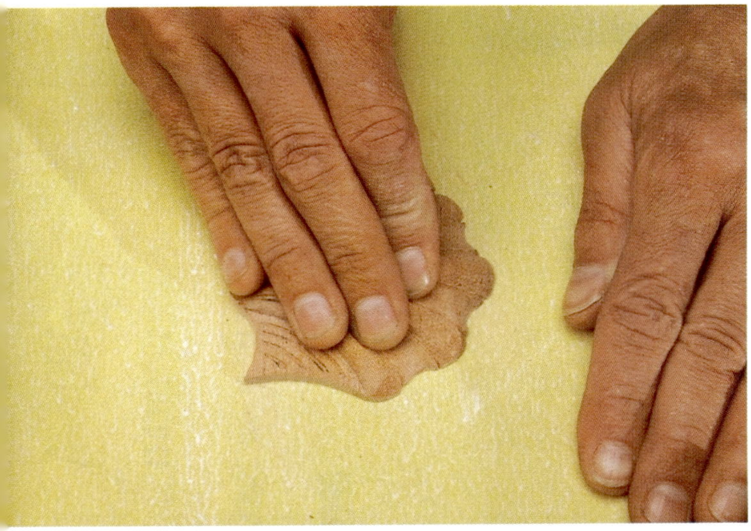

Sand the bottom of the piece, using a flat surface to support the sand paper. This not only gets any traces of glue off, it also gives a nice smooth sanding surface.

Roughly cut the shape of the shell you have drawn on the rail.

You want to leave the line, so it looks something like this.

Ready for joining.

Apply a liberal amount of carpenter's glue to the back of the shell.

Place the shell in place and squeeze as much glue out as possible by pressing down. You will notice that it tends to slide.

Spread it evenly with your finger. You want to be sure to have plenty of glue at the edges or it will chip with further carving.

Clamp the shell in place. I use a square of leather to protect the wood from the clamp. Tighten the clamp down as much as possible. This squeezes out even more excess glue.

Back the clamp off, and reposition the shell.

Bevel the back edge of the shield...

Retighten the clamp.

and the rail. This should bring it down to the shield.

We use a small scraper to remove the excess glue from around the shell. Do this while the glue is still wet. In a joint I would wait, but with a carving removing the glue while it is wet requires less pressure and creates less risk for the carving. I don't worry about the bottom edge, since it will be carved further.

Repeat on the other side.

The back of the rail should look something like this with the shield and the straight edges tapering in and down.

Mark the key points of the shell on the shield...

and carry the lines back. Then mark the areas to be removed.

Use a gouge to remove the wood, working from the back toward the shell. This is the safest way to do this without chipping the carving. The position we are working in is for illustration purposes. You can no doubt find a much more comfortable way to work.

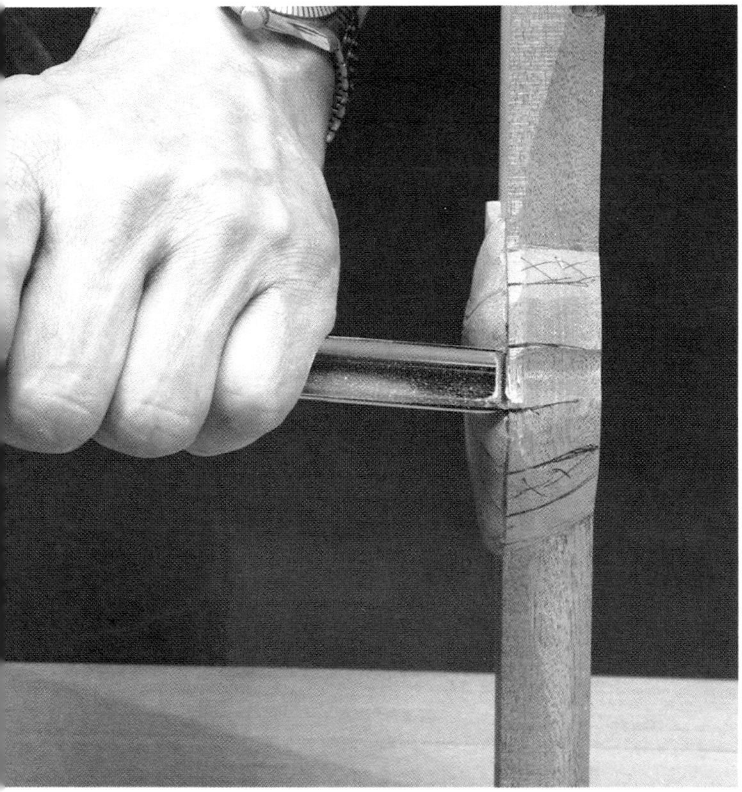

Return to the gouge you use earlier to set the shape of the shell, and score the rail by rocking the tip of the gouge back and forth. Gradually push it until the piece breaks off.

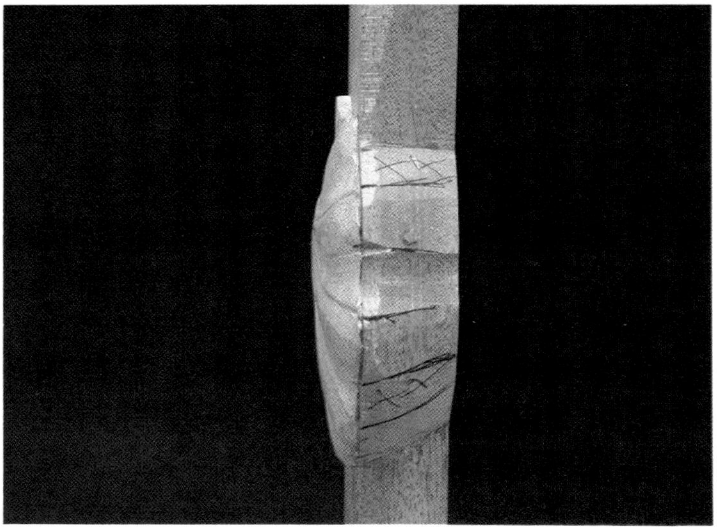

With a v-tool in the line of the shell, carry the line about a quarter inch into the rail

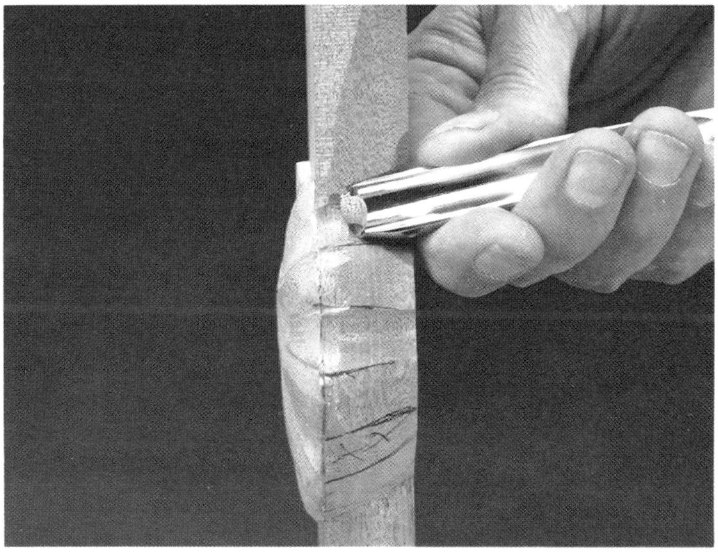

Repeat at the other valleys.

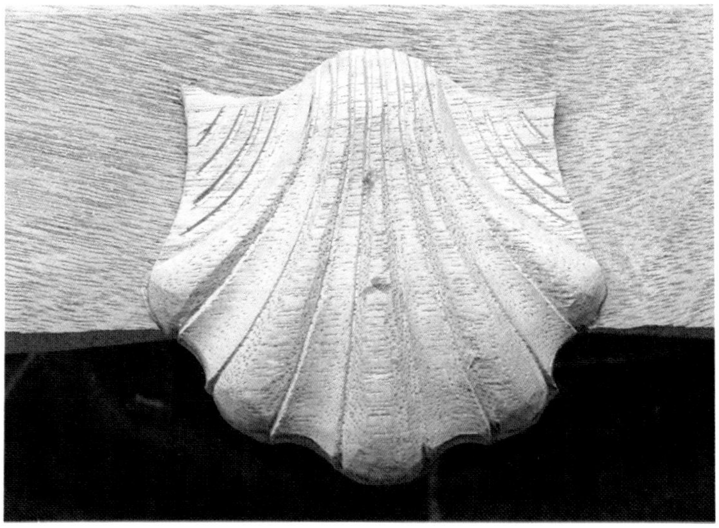

The shell in place, from the top...

and the edge.

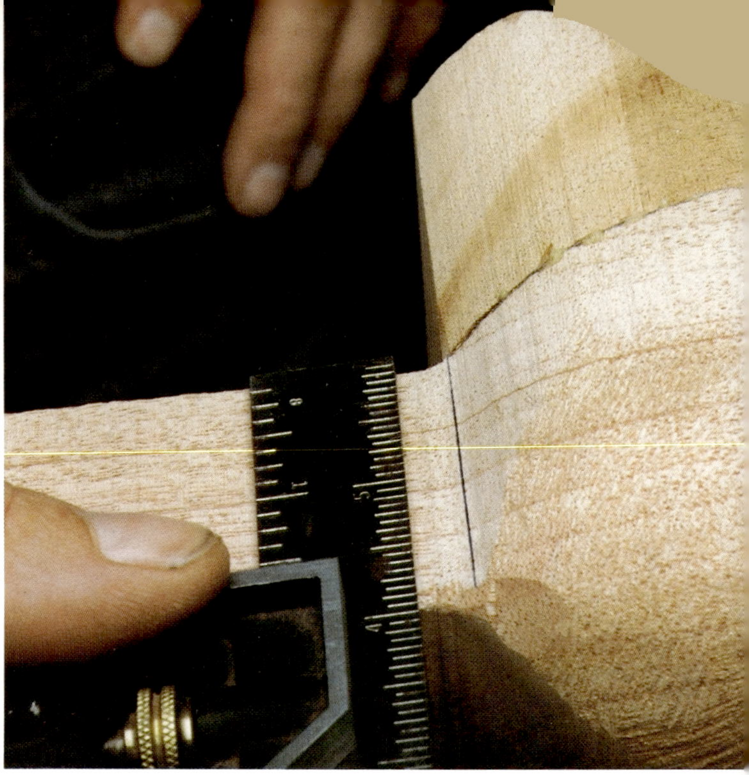

Mark the line of the shoulder, using the knee return as a guide.

Score the line with a back saw. Again, the knee return can be used as a guide for the saw.

Use a chisel to square the leg post, trimming back to the score line.

True the knee return with the knee across the glue joint. A chisel works well for this.

Continue down to the volute until you get to this point.

Draw in the corner shape of the post.

Turn the piece and repeat the process on the other knee return.

Cut a shallow stop in the corner where the post meets the knee.

Use the flat side of the rasp to chamfer the post edge. Start at the end of the post take the corner down to the mark. Carry the chamfer to about 1/8" above the stop at the knee. For now you want to keep this surface flat.

Nip off the last 1/8" with a chisel.

Go back and round off the edge.

Round the knee up to the post.

Use a piece of paper to find the center of the knee. Place one edge at one glue mark, and going across the widest portion of the knee mark the other glue line.

Lay the paper between the corner of the post and the center mark you have just made, and strike a line that is the vertical center of the knee.

Fold the paper in half to find the center and use it to mark the knee.

Measure a point 1" from where the bottom of the knee joins the knee return. Do the same on both sides.

Come from the glue line at that point and make a mark 3/4" toward the center of the knee. Do the same from both sides.

From that point measure a mark 4" down the center line. This is the length of the knee shell. A piece of paper has the flexibility you need to follow the curve of the knee.

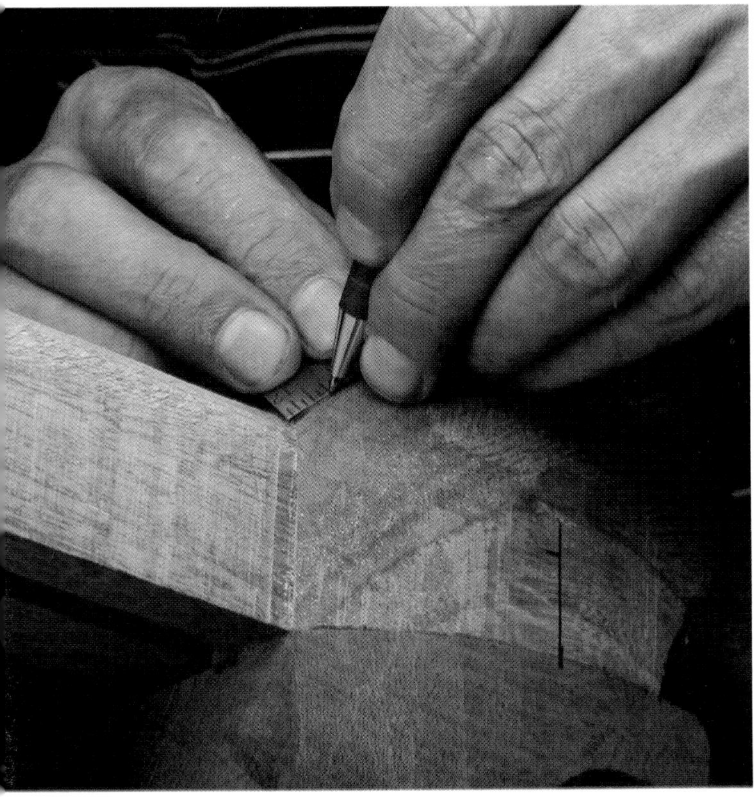

Make a mark 3/8" from the post on the center line.

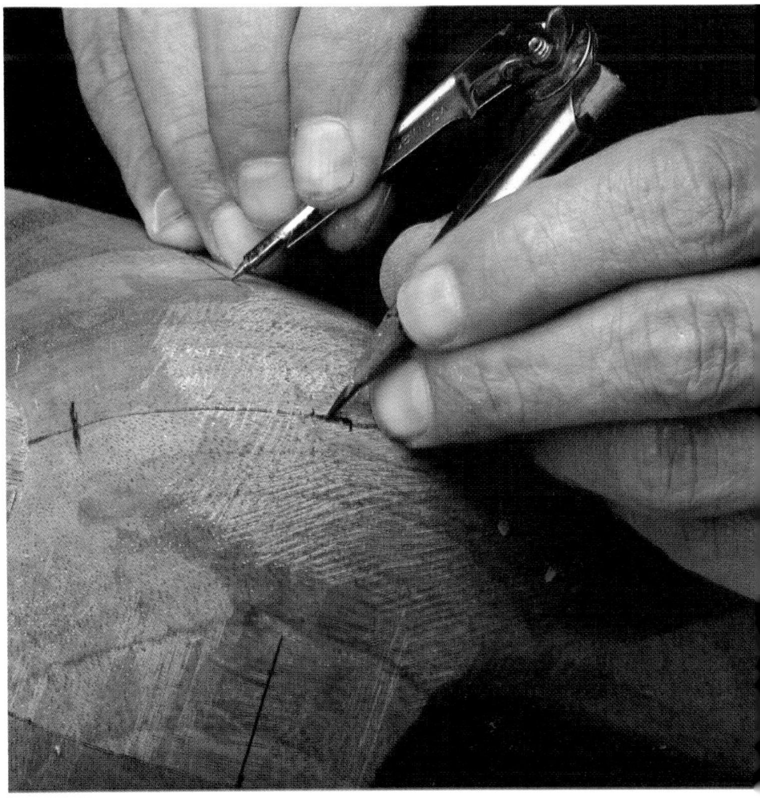

Take a compass and set its opening from the side mark to the center line.

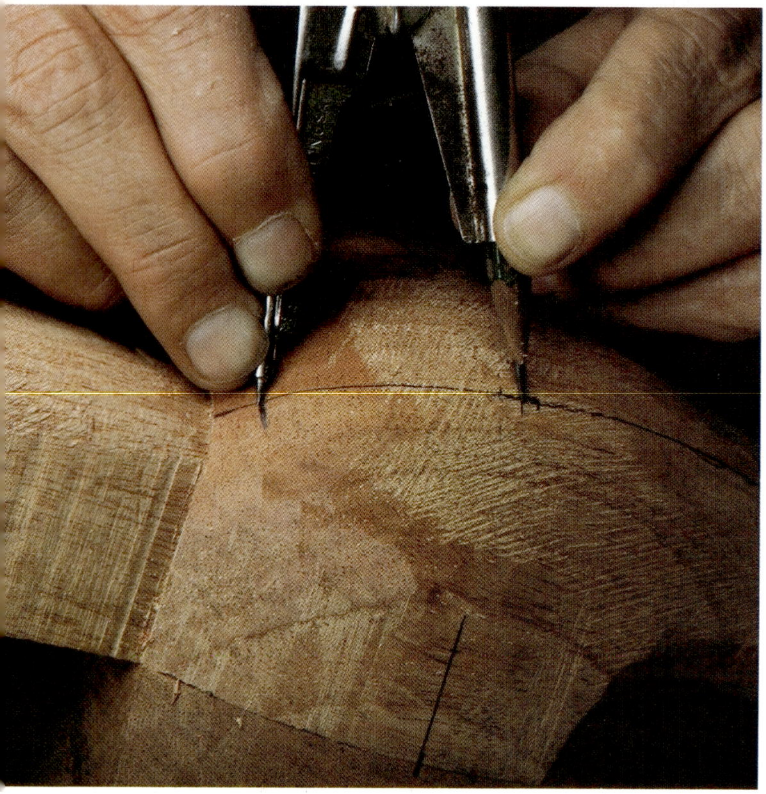

Move the point of the compass to the top mark of the shell and scribe a line across the center line.

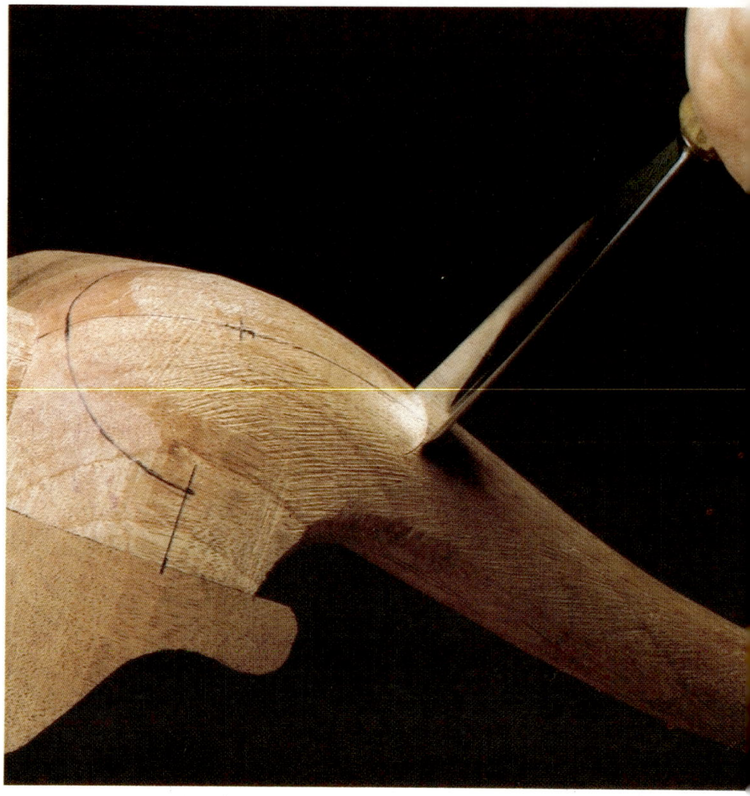

Mark the arc of the bottom of the shell by driving a No. 7 gouge into the bottom center mark.

Put the point in the center of the shell and mark the arc.

Find the point where the arc of the chisel cut is 1/2" from the center line and mark it on each side.

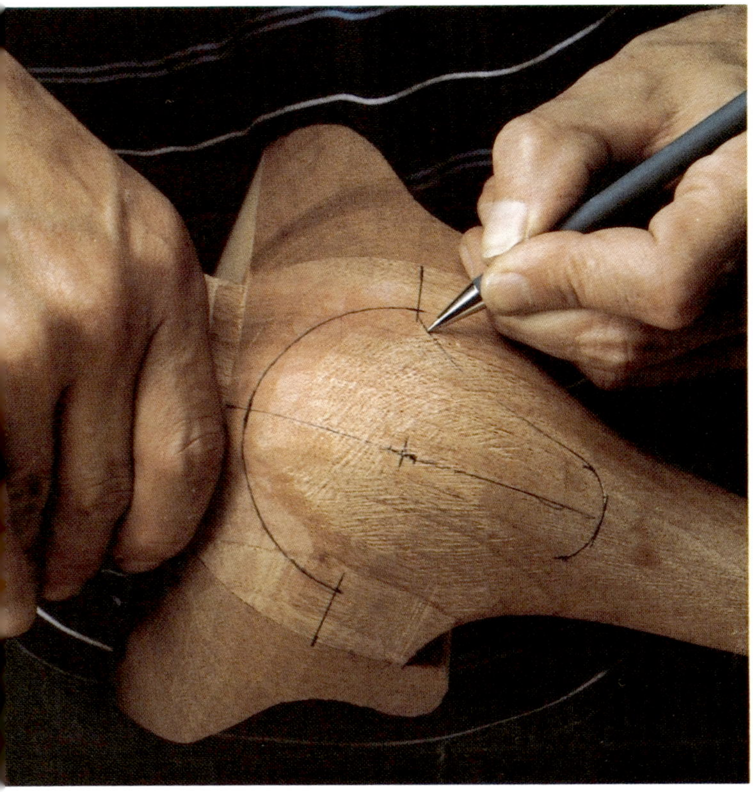

Draw the line of the side of the shell by connecting the end of the arc with the side mark. Because of the complex contours, this almost has to be done by eye.

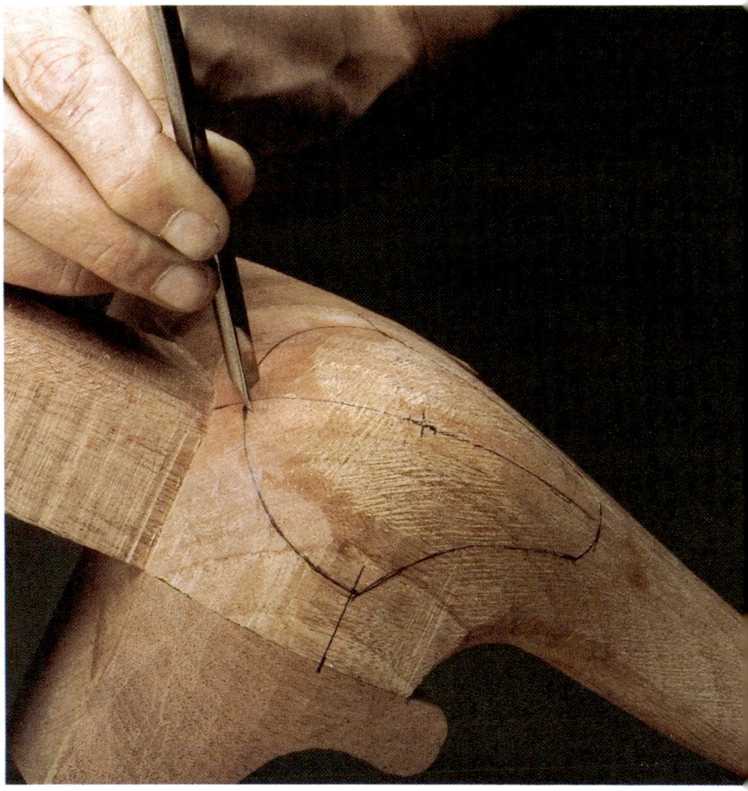

The final design of the scallop is based on a gouge width. With the approximate size drawn, you determine the actual size with a gouge, using trial and error. Choose a gouge that is approximately 1/9th the width of the scallop's arc. Begin with your gouge centered on the line, cup side down.

The outline of the shell.

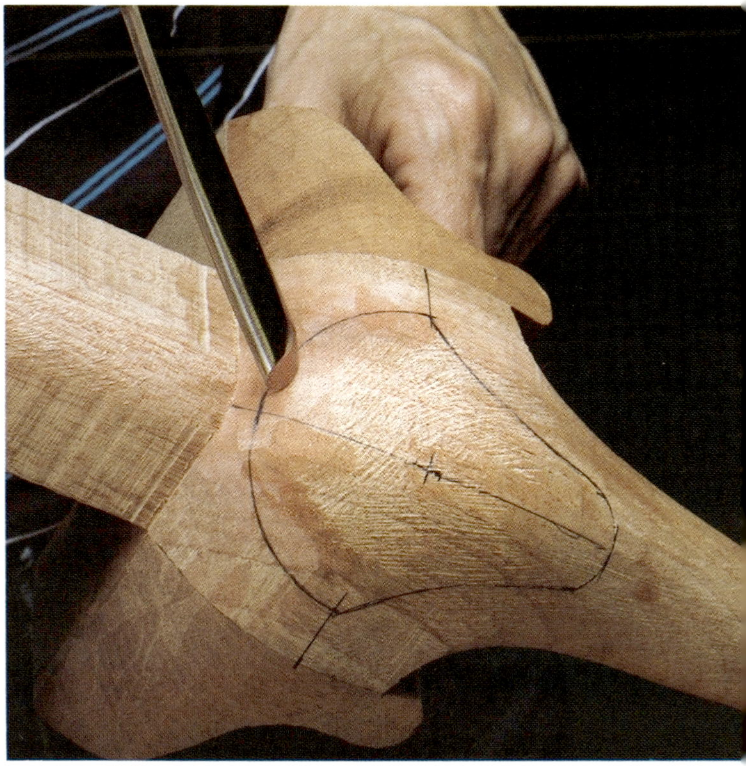

Walk the gouge out toward the outside. The first step will have the gouge side up...

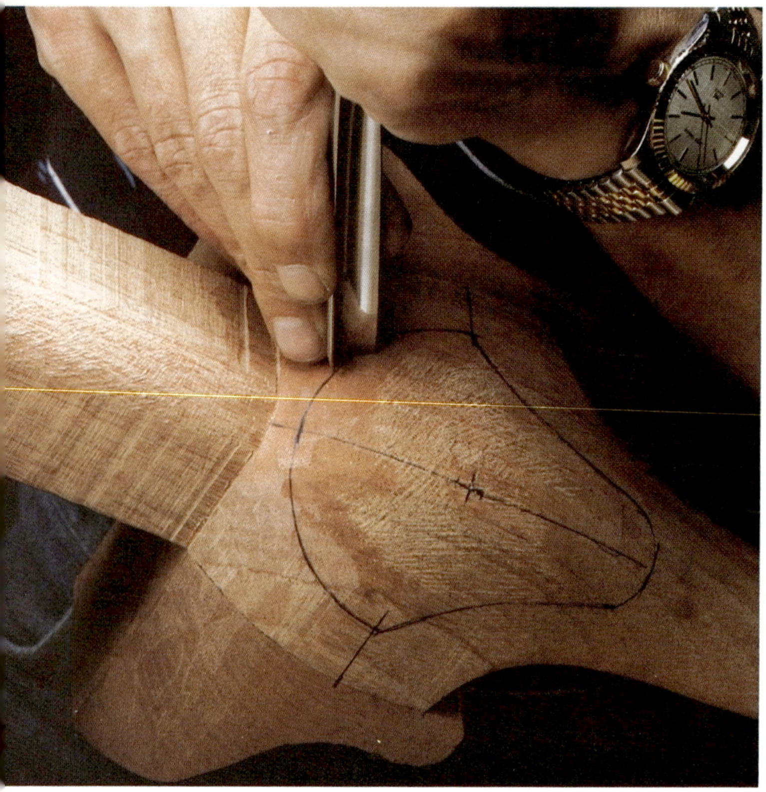

the next down...

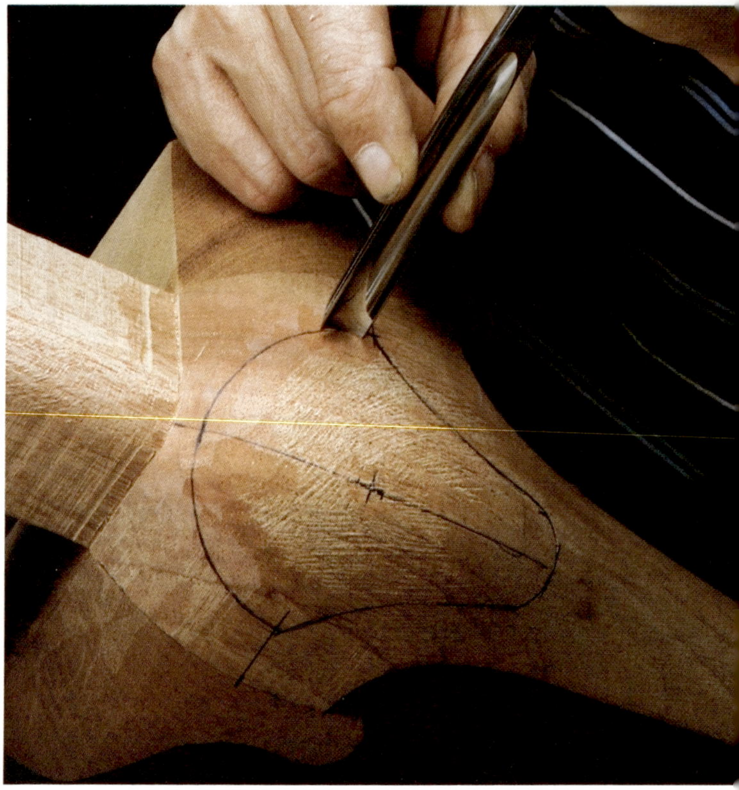

and the last down. If the last gouge position comes close to the line you have draw, it will be good. If not you'll have to try again with another gouge. This one is pretty good, and the last mark will define the edge of the shell.

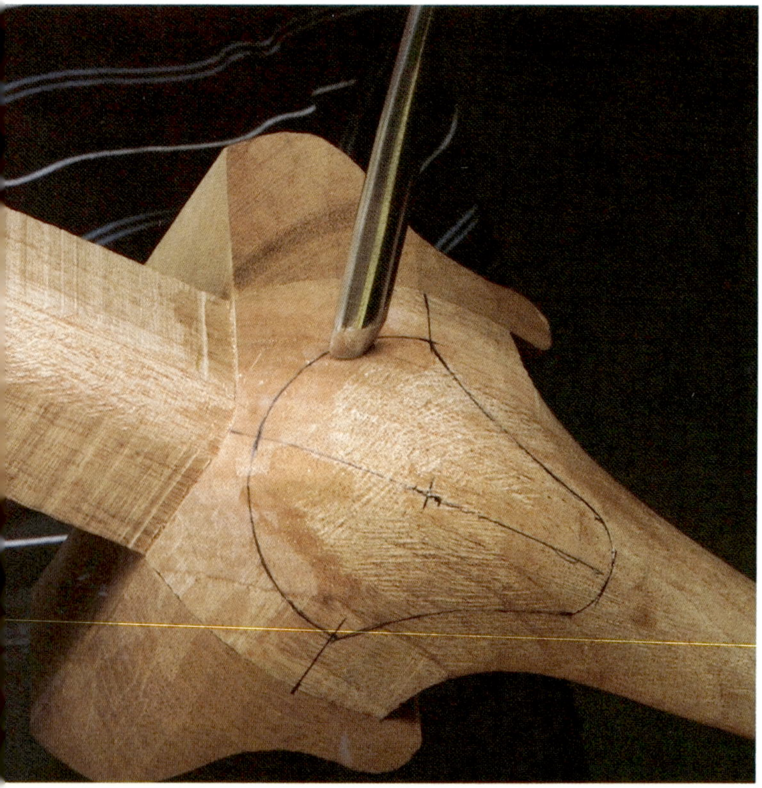

the next up...

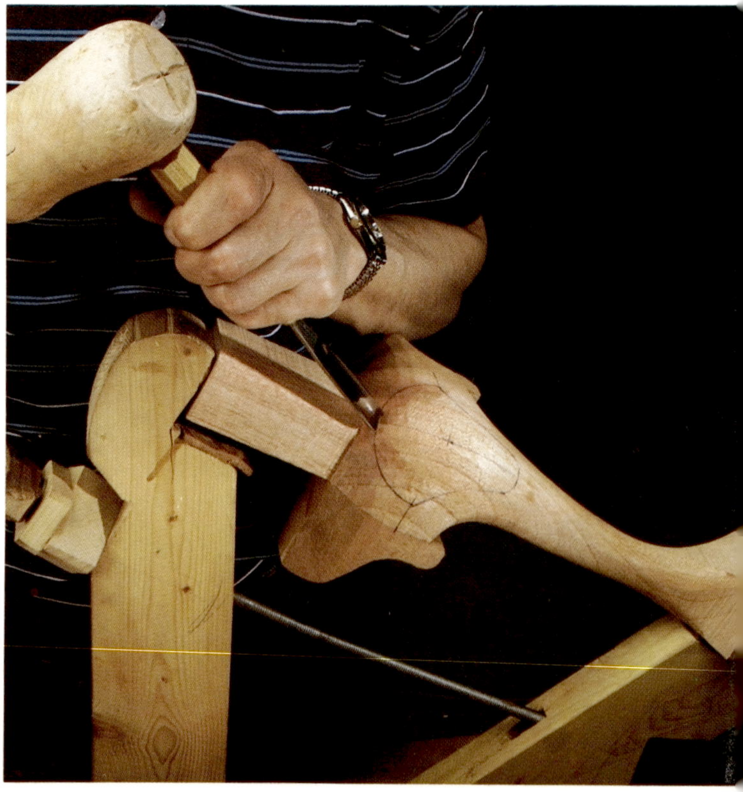

With the gouge width chosen, go back and define your line by driving the gouge straight in. Begin with it centered...

then walk it out as you did before, alternating the cup position.

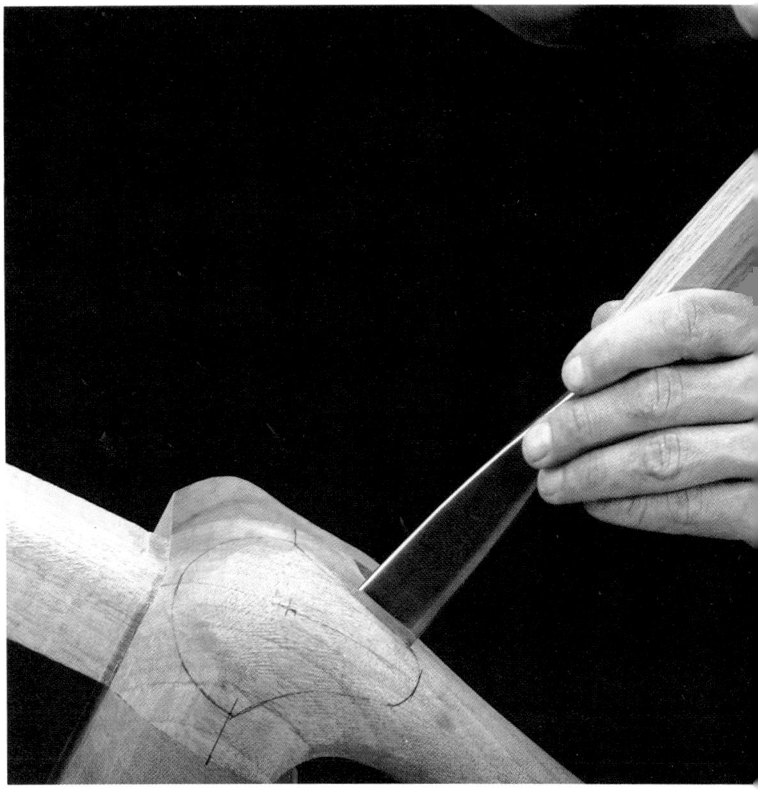

Use a gouge with a sweep that matches the arc of the lower side and create a stop by driving it in.

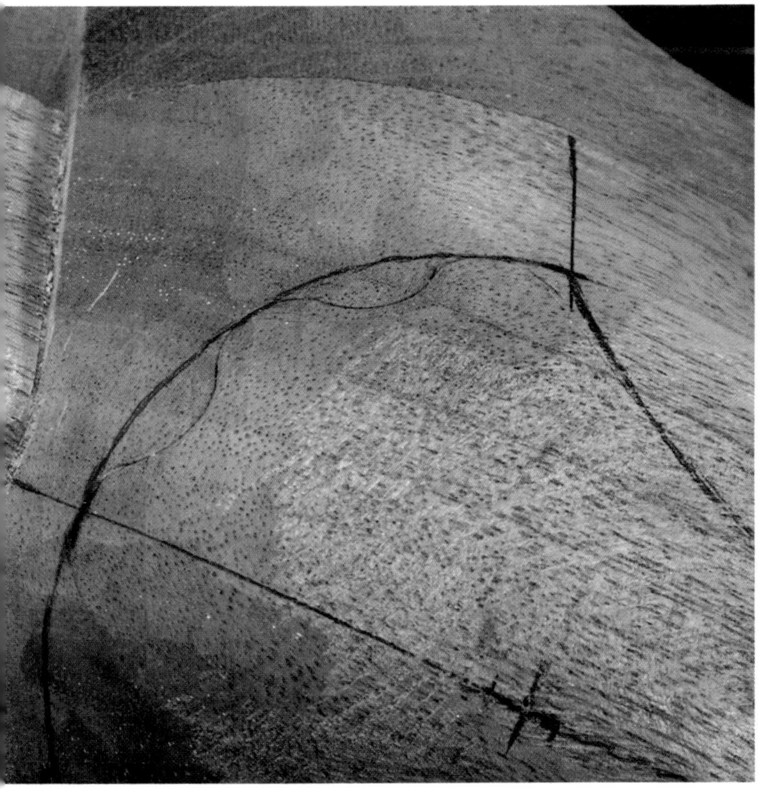

The emerging scallop pattern.

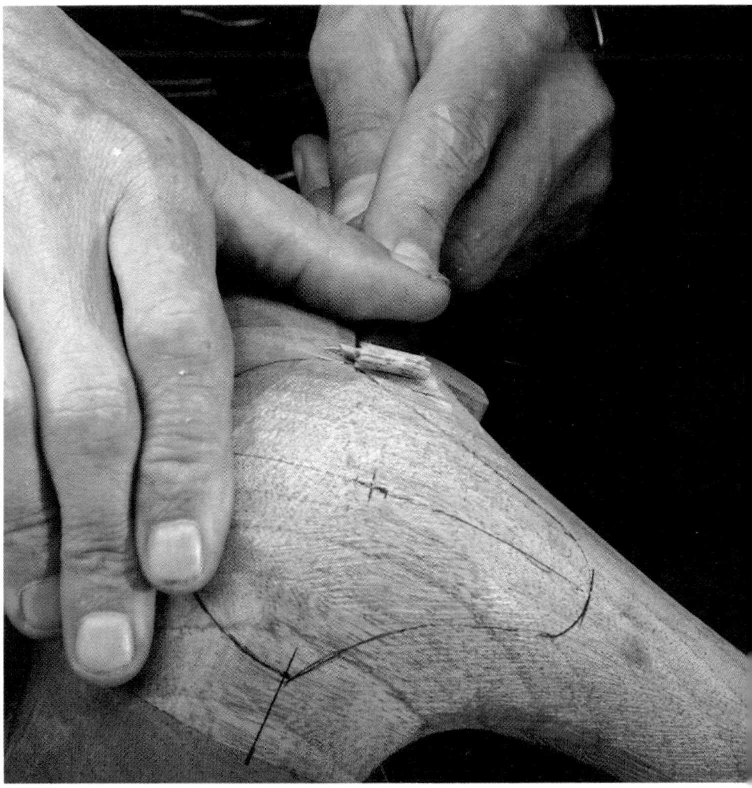

With the flat chisel, come in from the side and pare along the side of the shell. You will repeat this process going deeper each time until the shell "stands proud of the ground," raised a little more than 1/8" from the knee.

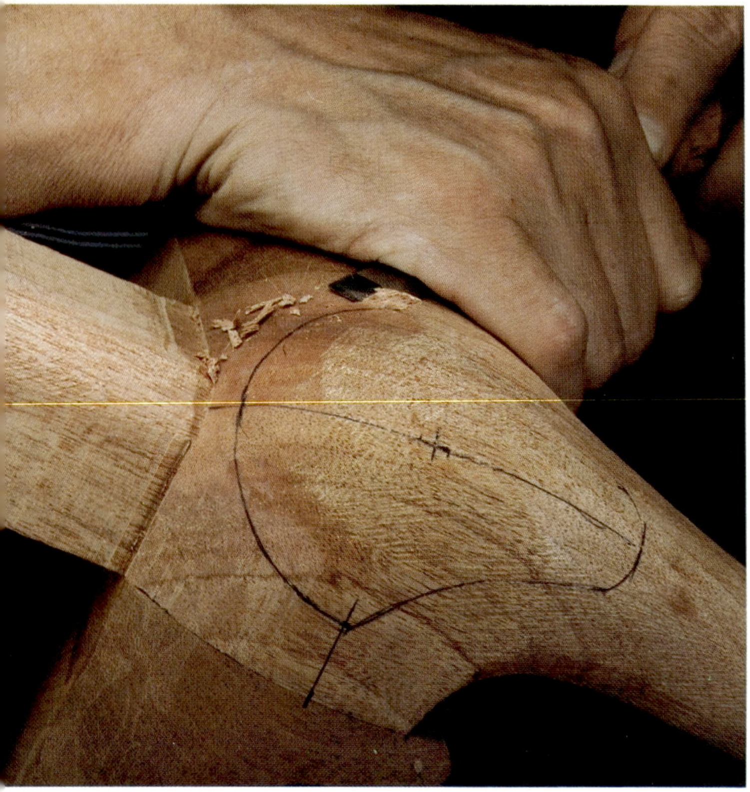

Go across the top of the shell with the chisel skewed so the corner goes against the scalloped lines.

Reset the lines on the scallop edge...

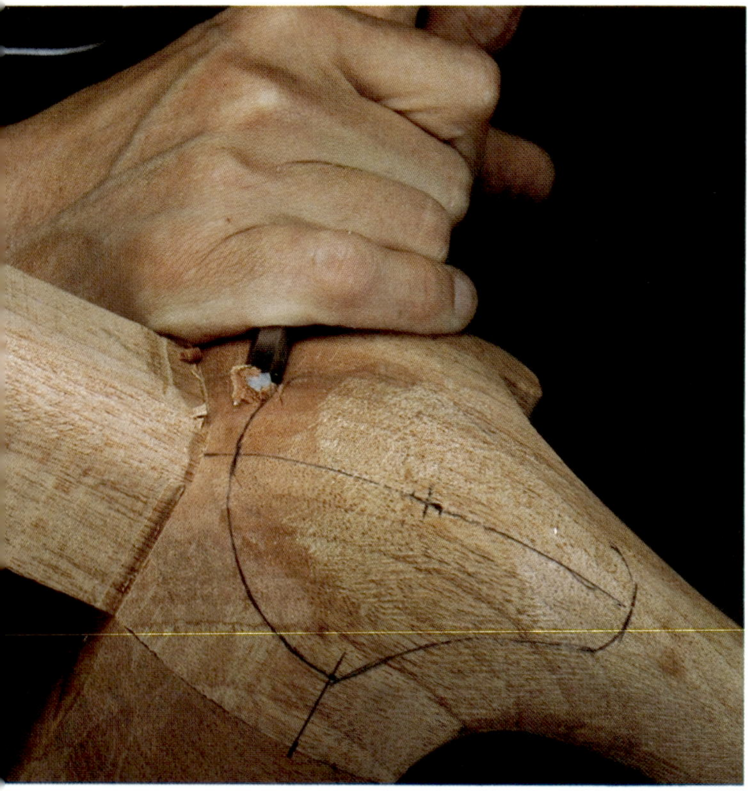

At the top of the shell we switch to a narrower chisel. This is end grain, so be sure the chisel is very sharp.

and the sides.

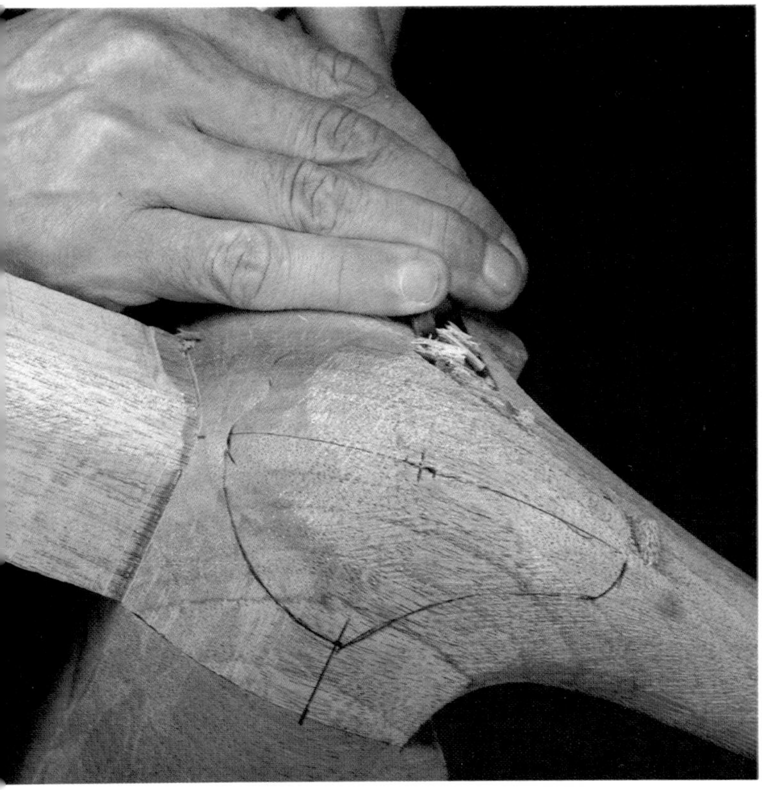

Trim around the shell. You want to keep the area surrounding as flat as possible, adding to the illusion that the shell is sitting on top of the leg.

Repeat the process on the other side.

Progress on this side.

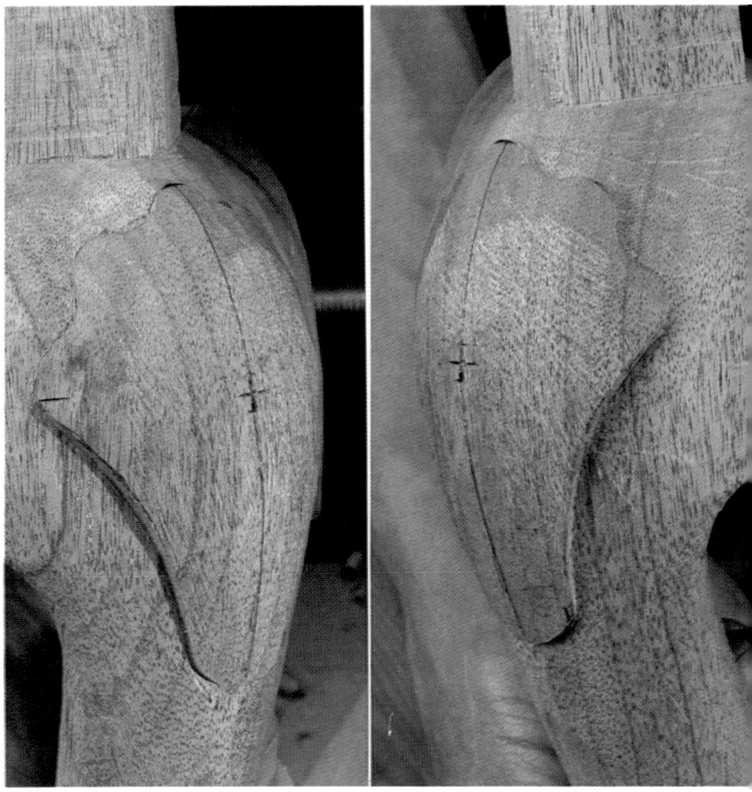

The shell is now set in and it is time to add details. The return is flush with the surface of the knee, and this is the final shaping they will get for the leg. There is however a little bit left at the top of the knee where it will meet the apron.

This line is where the apron will come. The wood in front of it will be trimmed after the stool is assembled.

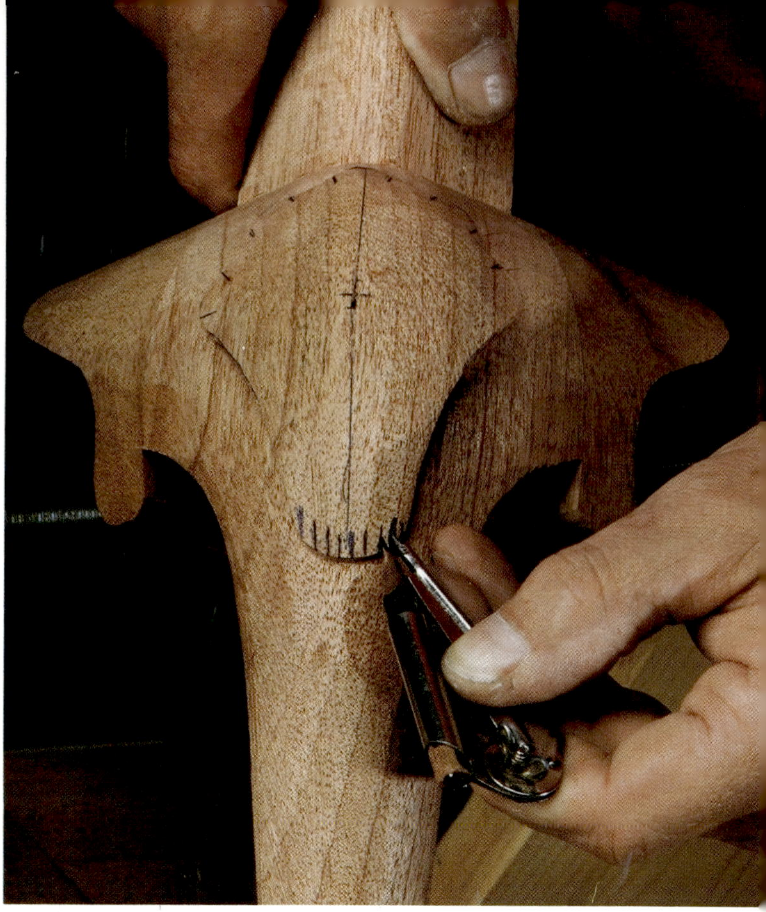

Do the same thing at the bottom. These 9 segments will be approximately 1/8".

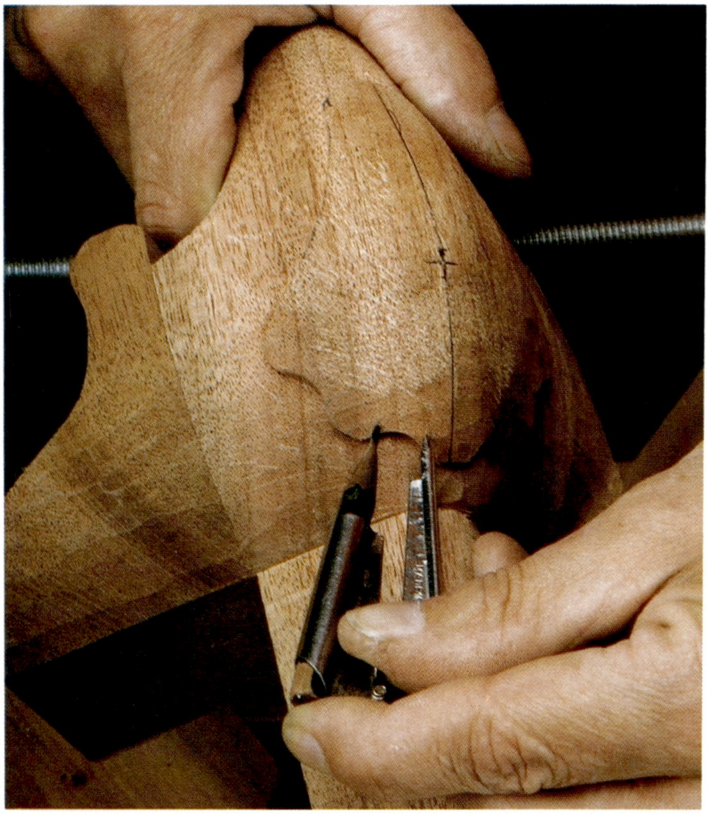

Set your divider so it will mark 9 equal segments across the top of the shell. This will require a little trial and error. When the divider is set, mark the segments from one side to the other. These will be approximately 7/16".

Sketch in the lines of the segments, by connecting the corresponding marks at the bottom and top. Use a nice sweeping line. These lines are only guides for the gouge. Permanent lines will be created later.

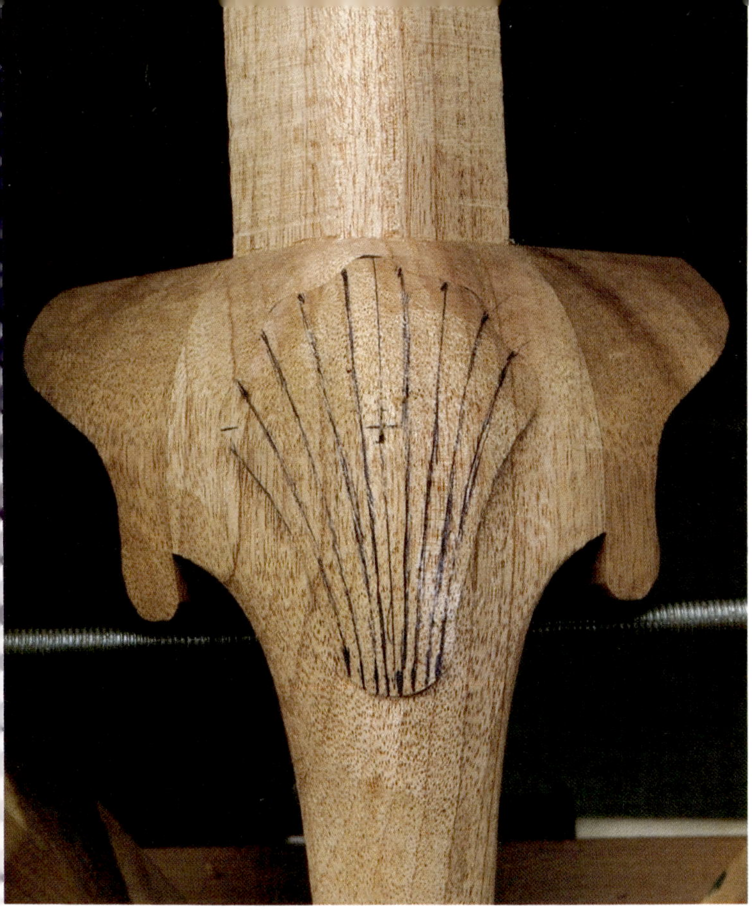

The lines drawn.

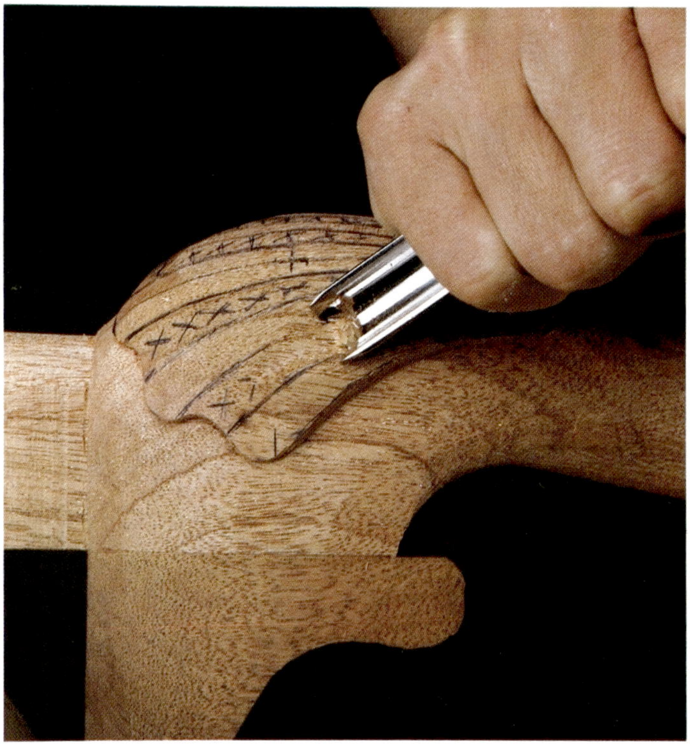

The process for carving the knee shells is very much like that for the flat shells, except the shell is curved, creating some different grain situations. Starting about a third of the way from the bottom, follow the valleys with a gouge (this is a 9/13). On the outside valley, you are going to run against the grain at some point and may have some tearing. A sharp tool and added care will minimize this problem. In any case, a slight tearing here is of no great consequence.

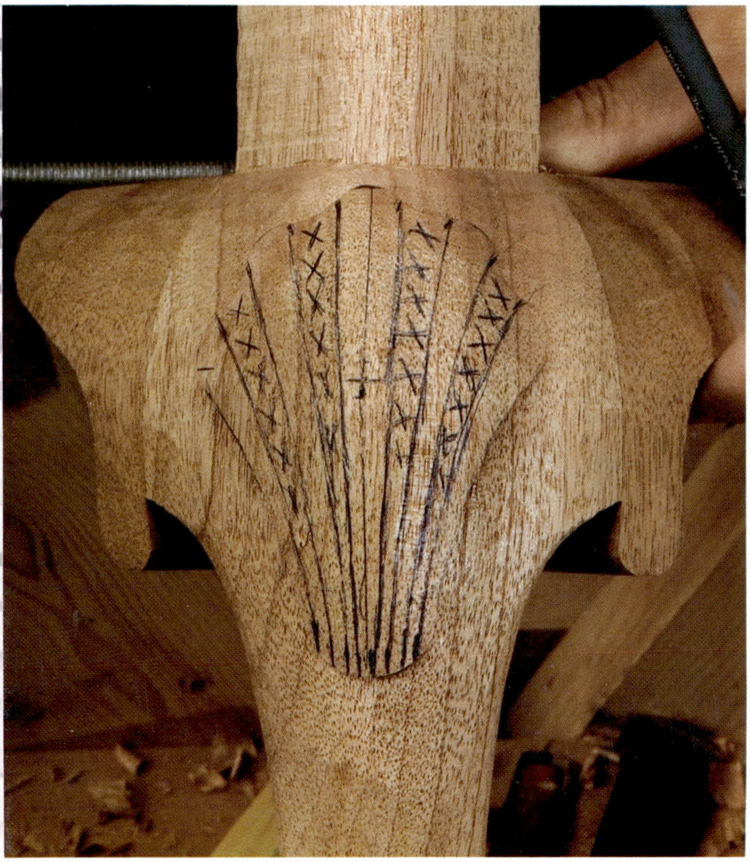

Mark the areas to be gouged for the valleys of the shell. As you get experienced at this, you probably will not need to use these marks, but for the beginner it is nice visual aid.

Switch to a gouge with a flatter sweep (this is an 8/13). Beginning about 3/4" from the top of the shell use this to widen the cut.

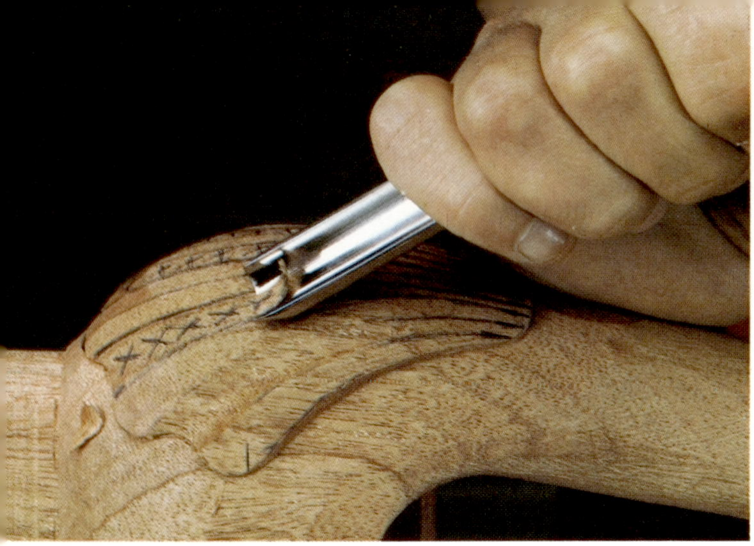

I always rough out one side of the shell before doing the other. This gives me the perspective I need to assure symmetry. Repeat the process on the next valley, beginning with the narrower gouge...

Now go back and deepen the valleys.

and switching to the flatter gouge for the end.

Round the ridges again. This time we'll use a flat chisel.

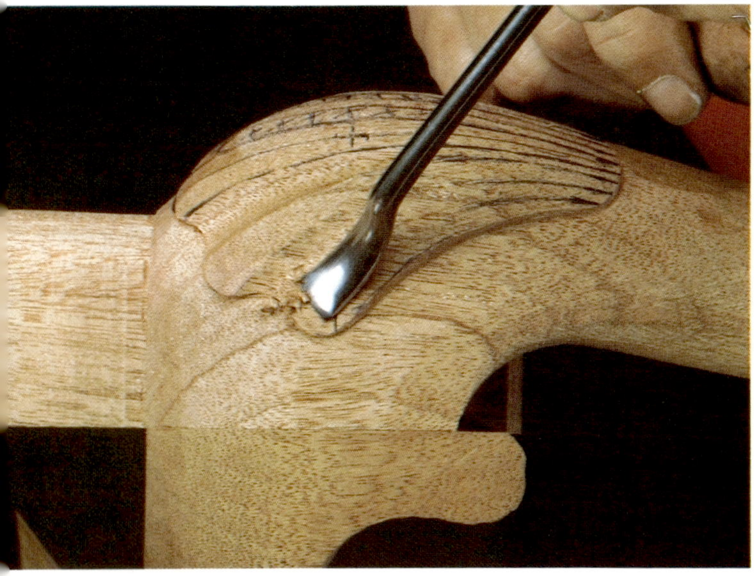

Do a preliminary rounding over of the ridges using a backbent chisel. You can do the same thing with a flat chisel.

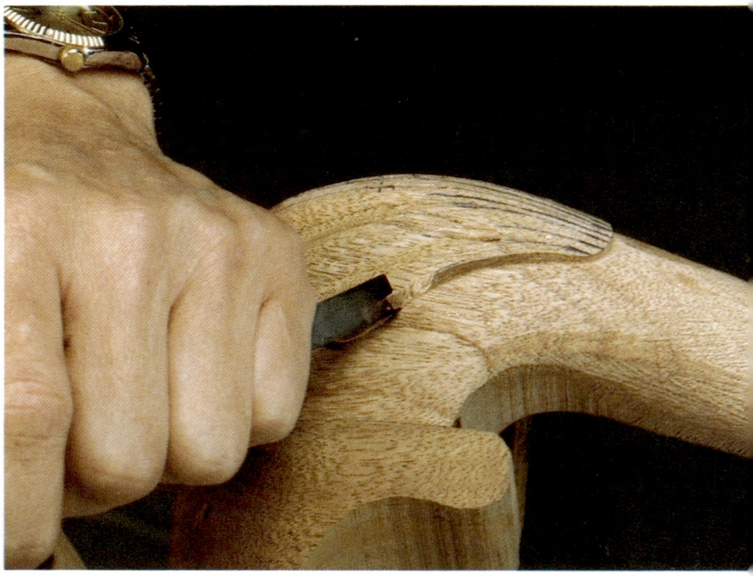

Because of grain direction, the outer edge of the outside ridges will need to be done from the top of the shell down.

With one side roughed out, I am ready to do the other.

Follow the same basic steps, referring to the finished side to assure symmetry.

The top of the shell is carved.

Redraw the lines of the shell. These are the reference lines for cutting the rays of the shell.

The rays are cut with 12L/6 long bent parting tool. Simply follow the lines, starting about 1/3 of the way up the shell...

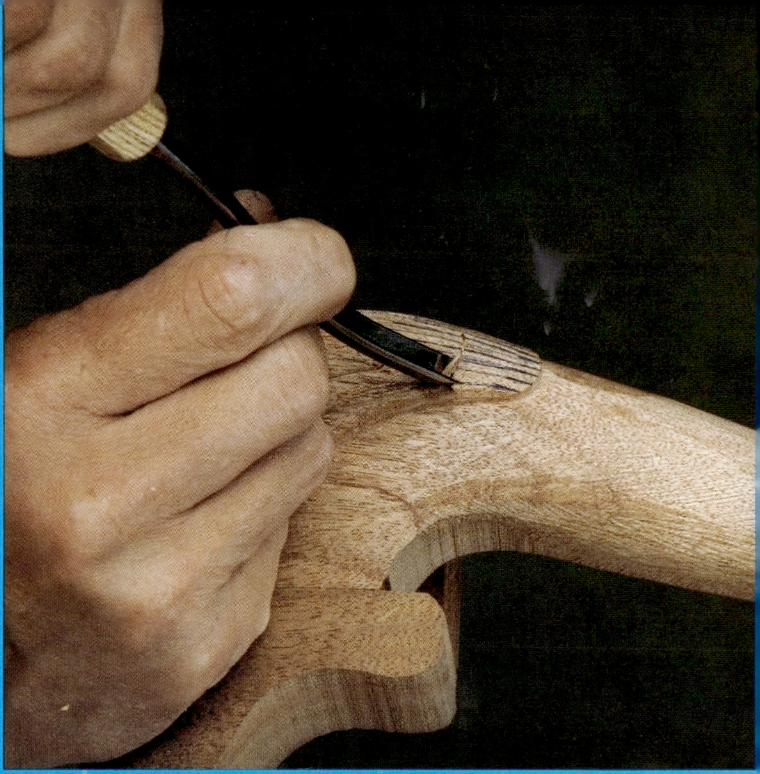

When the upper rays are cut, turn and do the lower part. Simply place your tool in the groove you've cut and go to the bottom.

and carving to the top. These rays cuts need even pressure, and are best when done in one stroke.

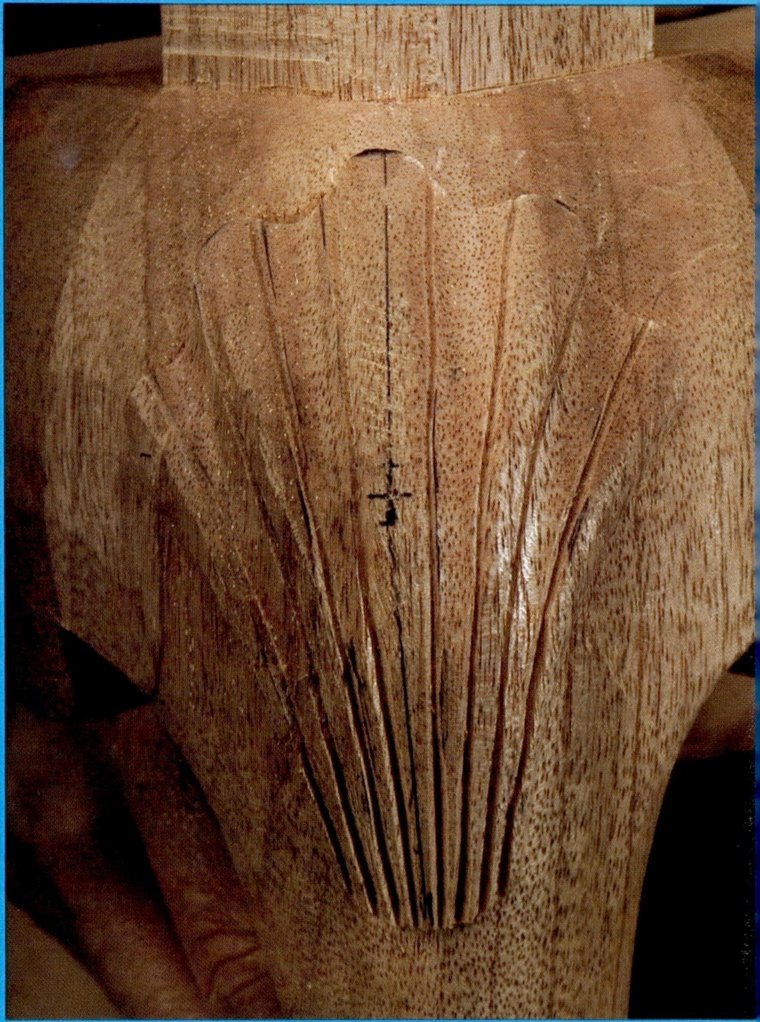

The carved rays.

Round the ridges into the rays you have carved. Be careful not to nick the groove.

You need to watch your grain, and reverse your direction where necessary to avoid chipping.

The shell is now ready for final sanding and finish.

Clamp the leg to the bench to carve the volute.

This is the basic design for the volute carving, though it may vary from piece to piece.

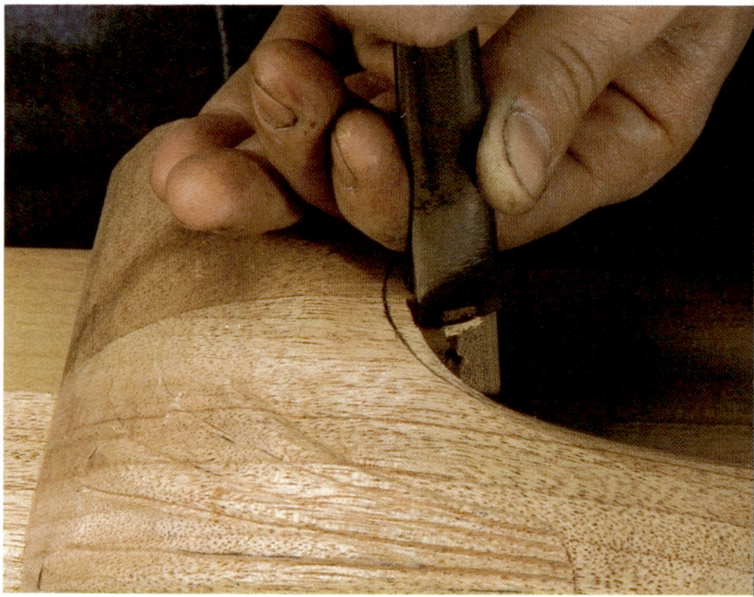

We need to round up the knee return around the volute pattern. You can use whatever tool will work. We'll use a fairly flat gouge. Go all the way across the underside of the knee return.

Refer to the template and draw the pattern on the volute. Notice how the curve is continued to the underside of the knee. These are guidelines, and you need not follow them exactly.

Continue all the way around. The alignment is done by eye.

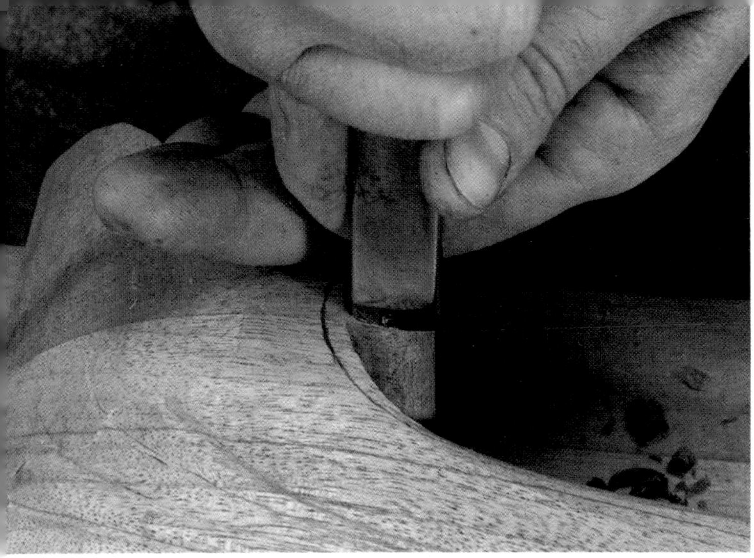

When you have established the shape, go back and smooth things up.

We'll use a series of number 7 & 8 gouges to carve the volute. They have different sweep and widths for different parts of the volute's spiral. Choose the gouge by how it fits the curve.

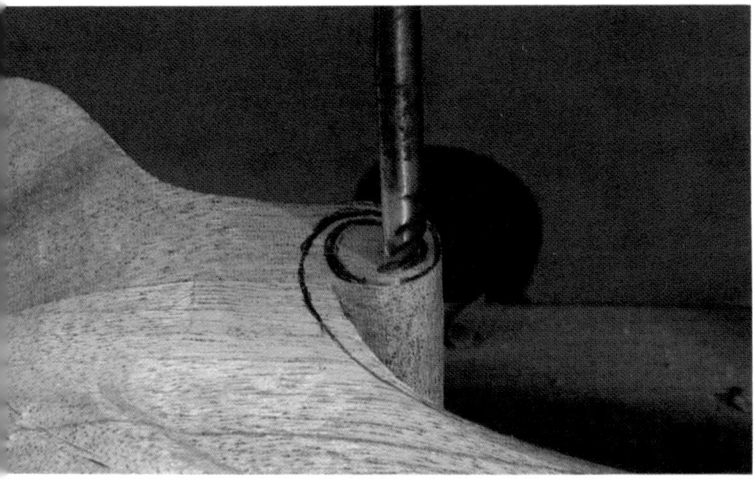

Begin at center of the spiral, where the two lines converge. Press a narrow No. 7 gouge along the inside line. You want to keep the chisel angled so it cuts into the incised spiral, and does not undercut the surface.

Continue along the inside line by pressing a No. 8 gouge. Overlap a little bit with the previous cut to insure that the patterns are cut.

Continue working your way around the spiral. We can continue to use the No. 8 to this point..

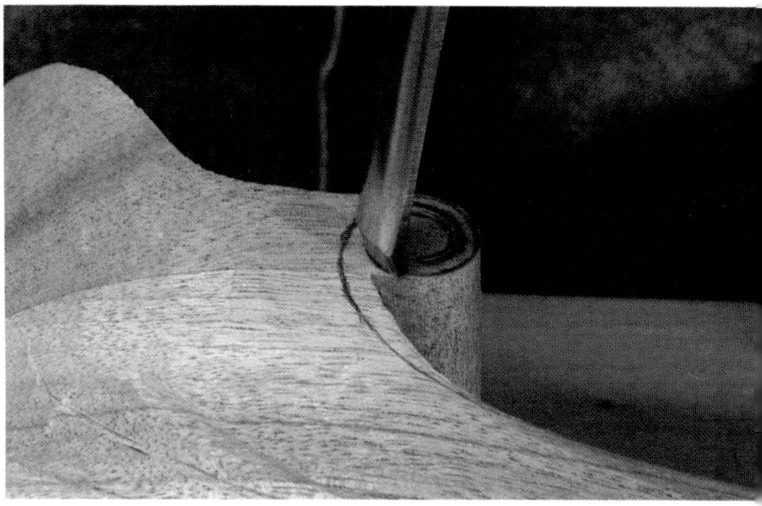

before switching to a flatter, wider, No.7. Remember these gouge selections are for this particular spiral, and may vary on your piece. Pick the gouge that best matches the line. This seven takes us to the outside.

You may wish to bring the gouge around the outside of the volute, just to round it up.

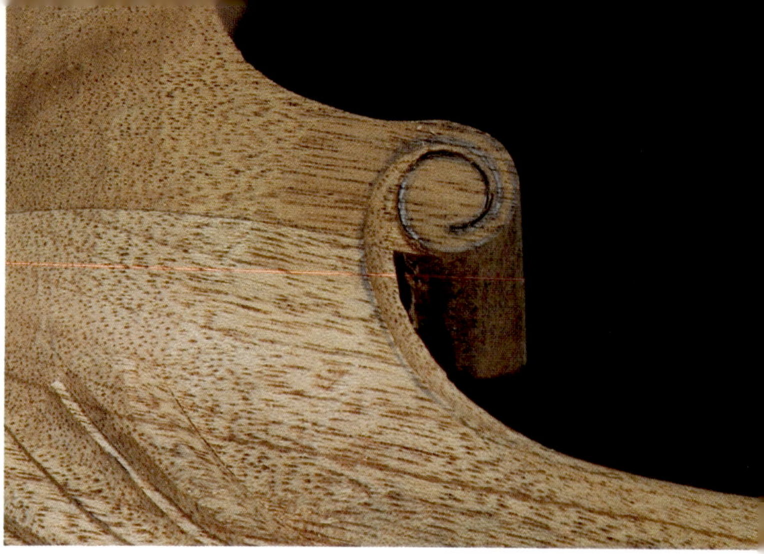

Progress report.

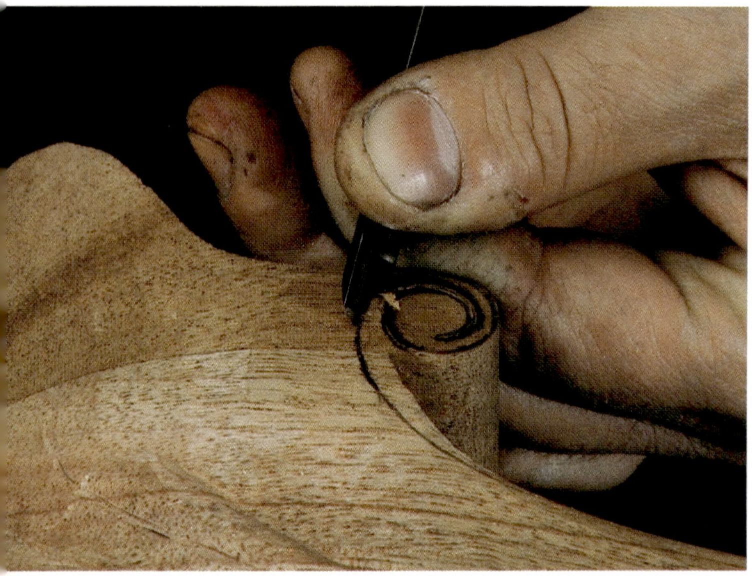

About half-way around the spiral use a flatter no. 7 gouge to slice along the outside line. The slice will slope back to the more vertical stop you just made along the inside line of the spiral. Use a nice, flowing stroke.

With a wider No. 7, begin at the point where you began the outside slice, and push from the outside line, down and back to the vertical stop on the inside curve.

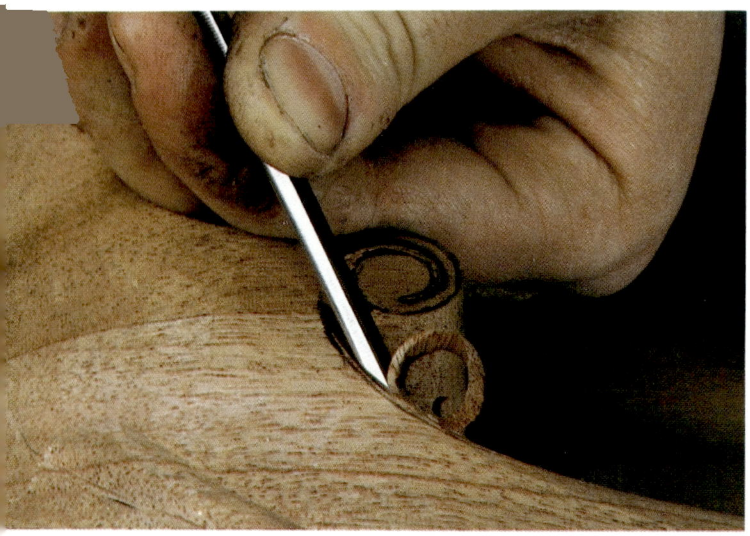

Continue onto the leg where the curve blends with the line of the leg.

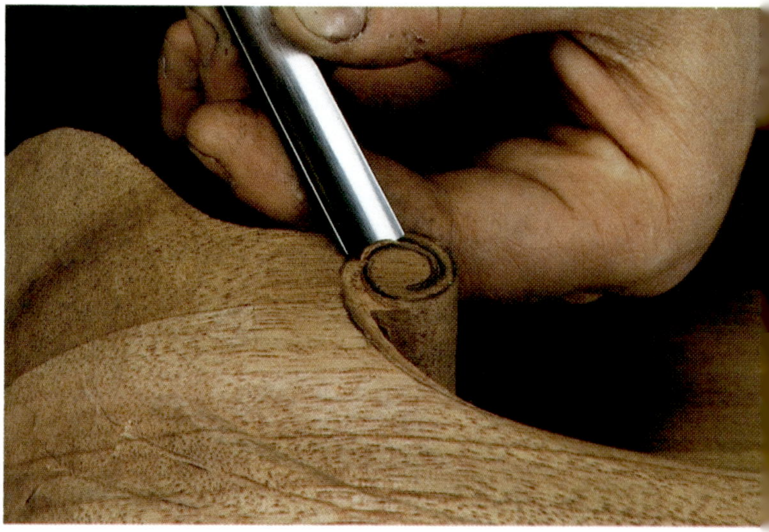

When the you reach the stop, the slice should pop right out.

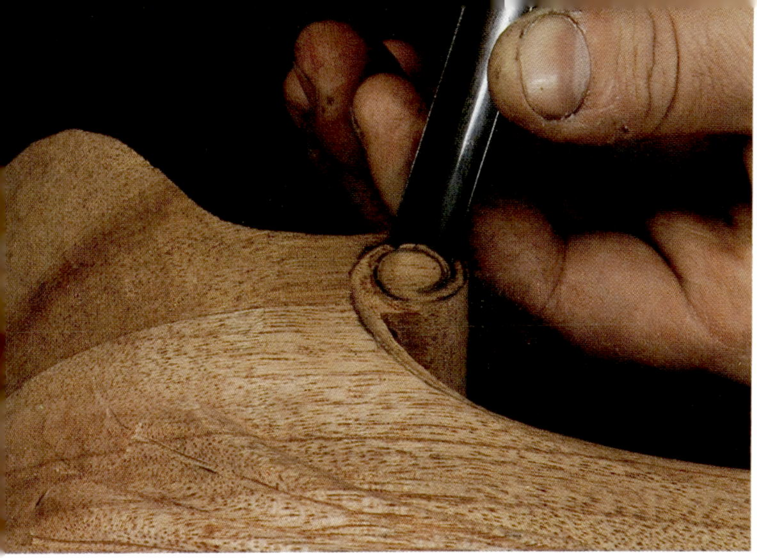

Work your way toward the point of the spiral, using this method.

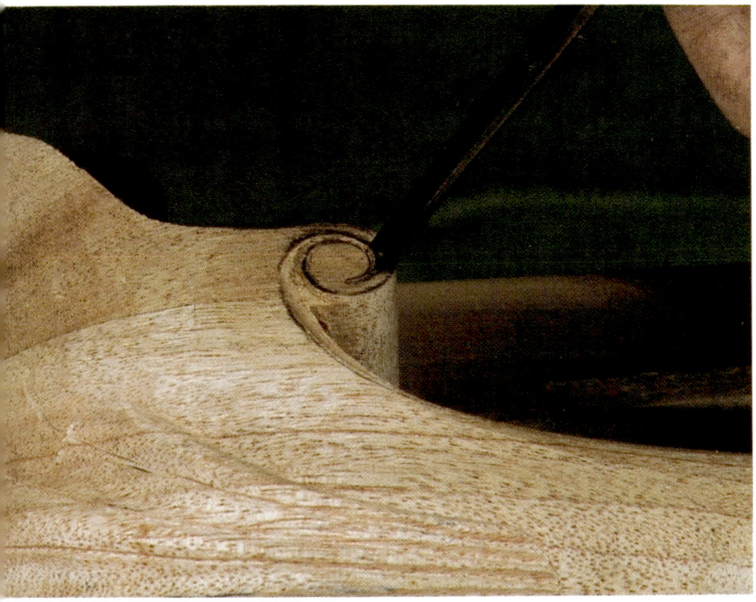

Switch to a narrower gouge as the spiral tightens.

Move step-by-step...

until you reach the beginning of the spiral. The spiral is shallowest at its beginning, and gets deeper and wider at its end.

We need to take the bevel of the volute about this deep to give it the illusion of being a curved piece of wood.

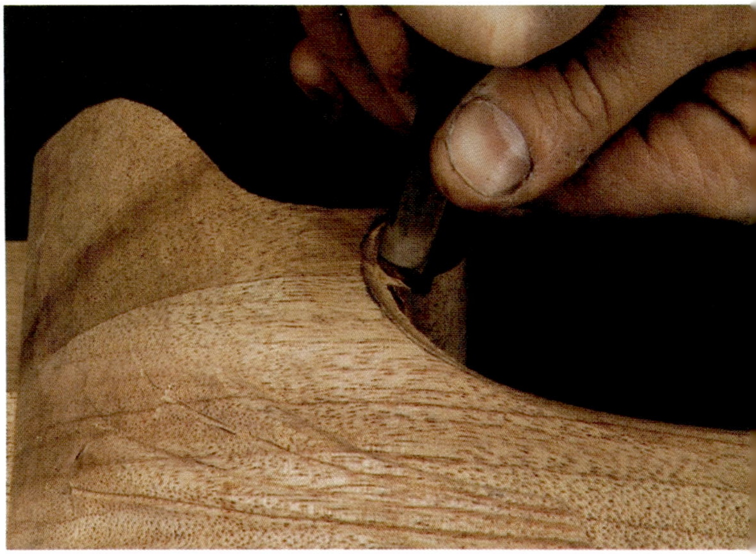

With a No. 7 gouge deepen the stop that defines the outside of the volute by pushing straight in.

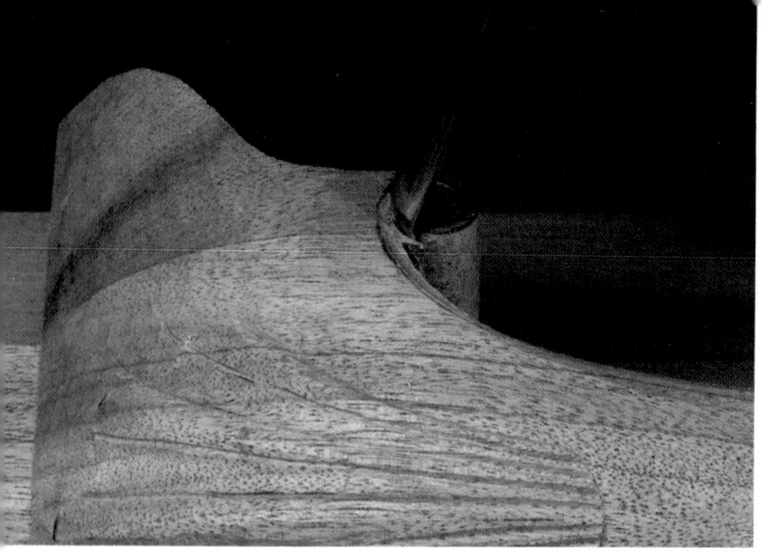

Continue this stop around the volute, gradually decreasing the depth.

To deepen this bevel, take a wider, flatter gouge...

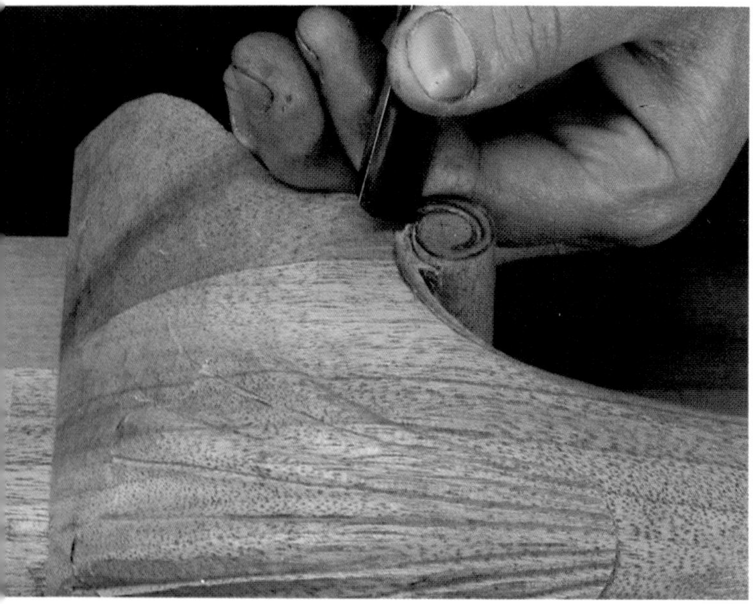

start about here...

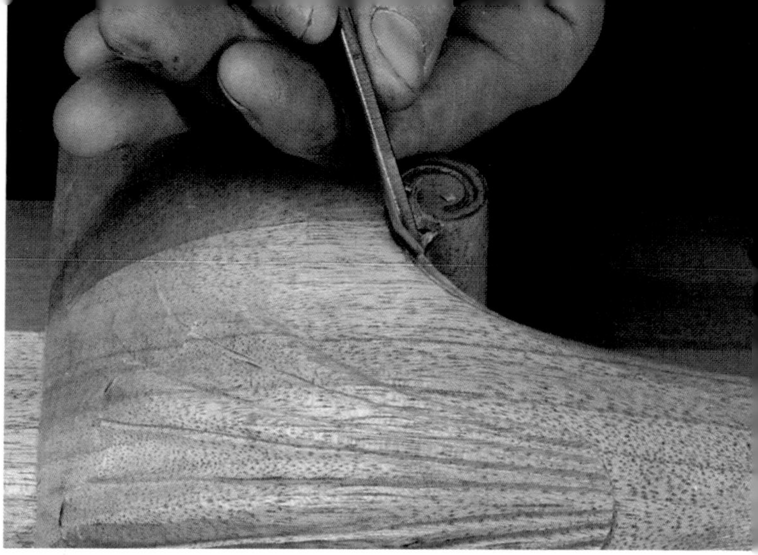

and deepen the sweep. Slowly turn the tool up in one continuous stroke. The blade angle starts at about 45 degrees and ends up at about 90 degrees. This means that, as you come down the leg, you are not trimming the edge, but undercutting it. Your original line should be pretty much intact.

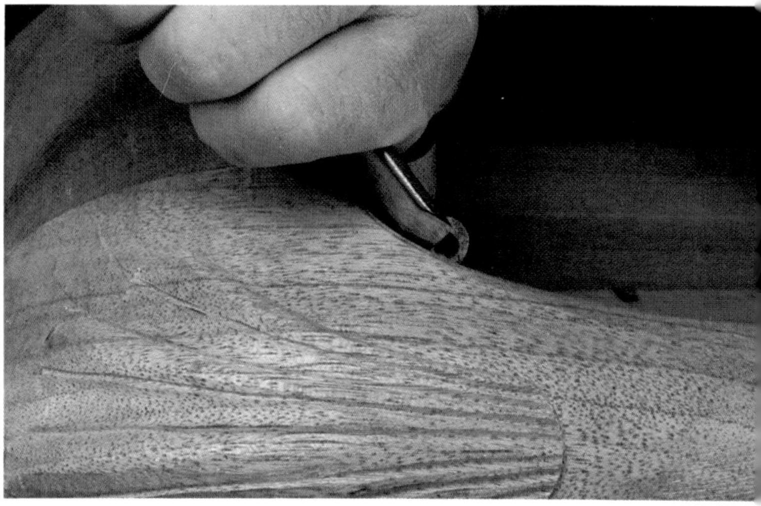

As you reach the end, you should be blending with the leg.

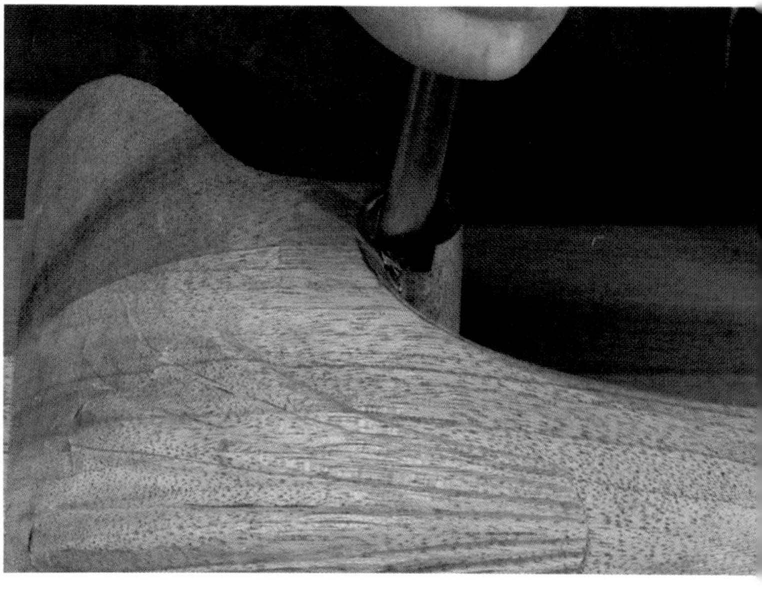

Repeat the process a couple of times, deepening the curve of the volute...

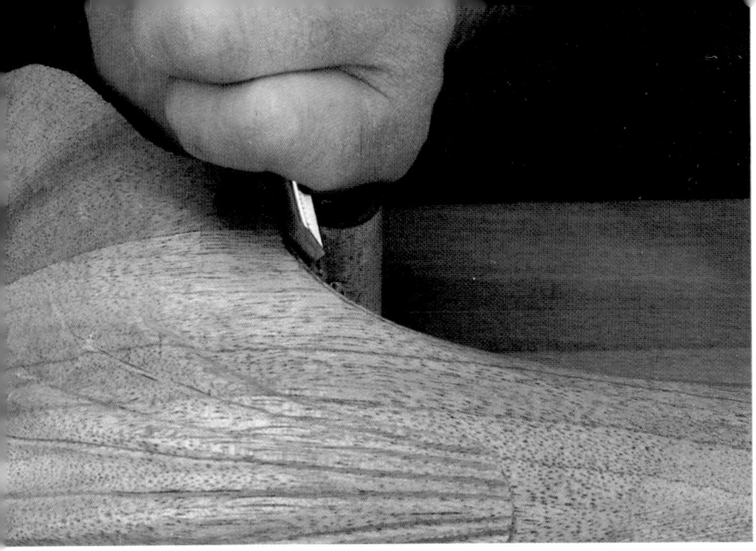

and slicing around the spiral.

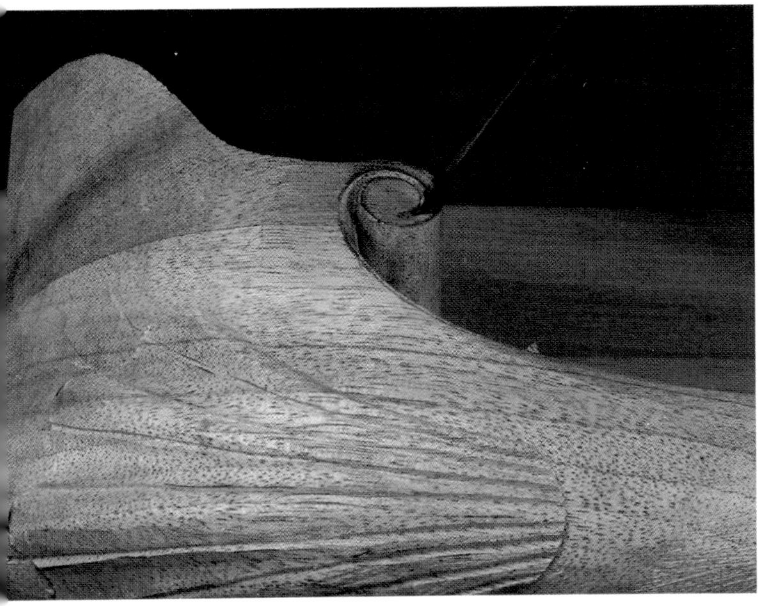

Continue deepening the spiral toward its beginning.

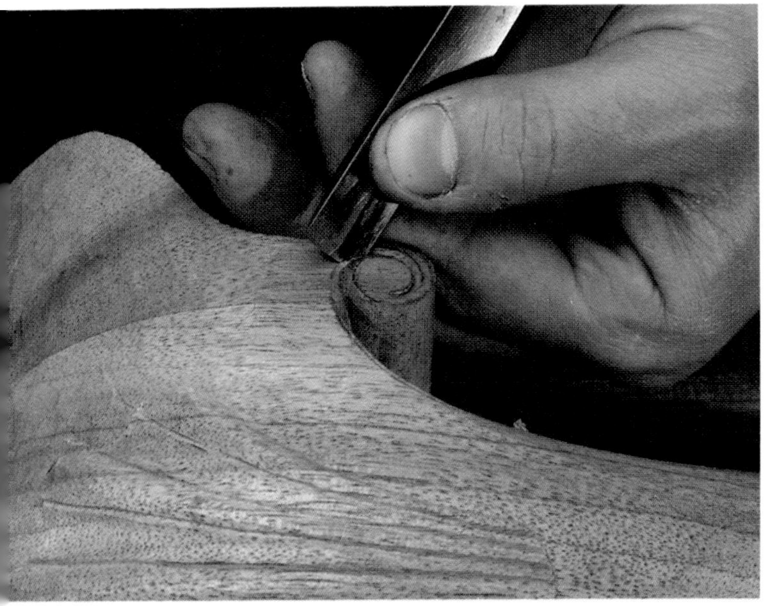

Go back and clean up the spiral.

The carved volute. Repeat on the other side.

A pattern maker's file does a nice job of taking away saw marks on the under side of the knee and knee return. Use the flat surface for convex curves...

and the rounded side for the concave curves.

You may wish to taper the surface toward the back. To give an added sense of dimension and grace to the piece.

On the volute, smoothing can be done with a wider gouge. This is a No. 5. A flat chisel can also be used.

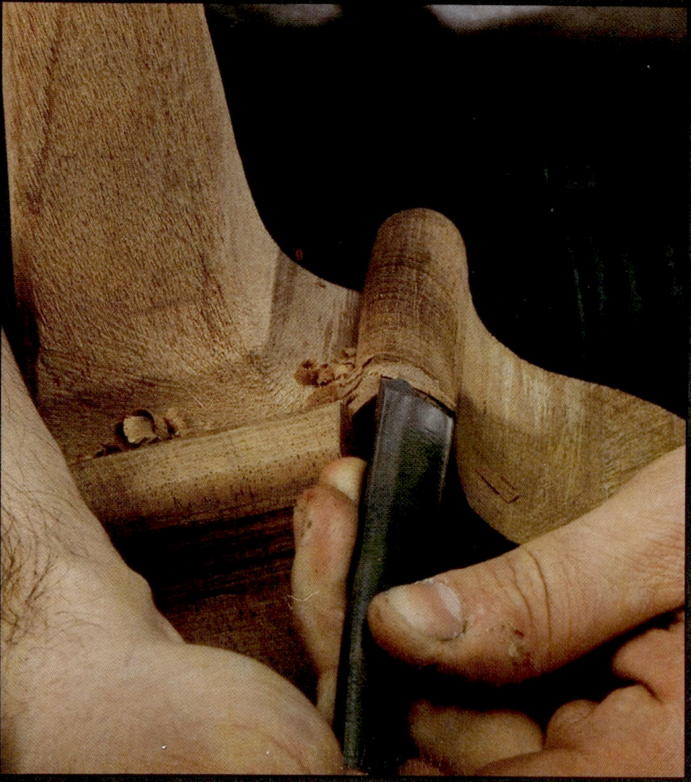

At the end of this trimming you must be careful not to simply break it off. Come at it from the side or from the opposite direction.

Blend the lines under the knee.

Go over the underside of the knee with a file or chisel to get rid of the bandsaw marks.

The finished knee area.

Lay the pattern on the bottom of the foot.

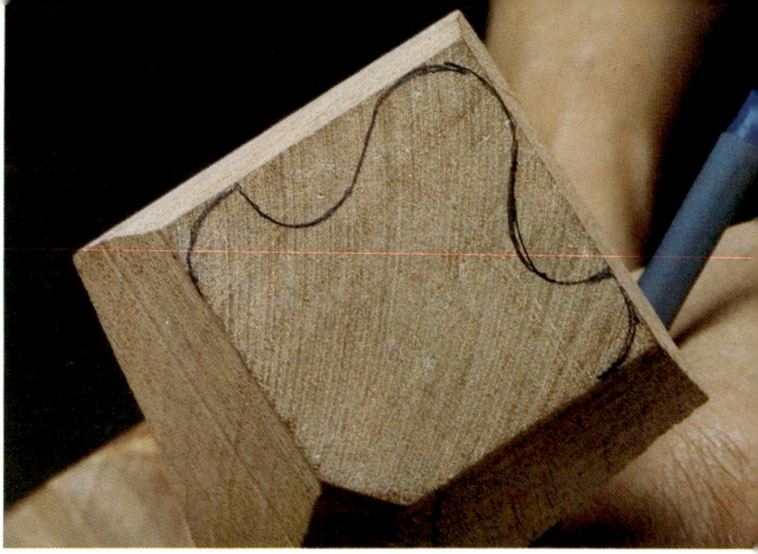

The drawn pattern.

Mark one side...

From the inside line of the toe measure 1/8" and make a mark.

then flip it over and mark the other side.

Use a finger and the pencil to transfer the depth of the line...

to the top of the foot.

Connect the marks.

Make a mark on each side at the points of the back toes.

On the upper surface of the foot draw an arc to define the back of the toe.

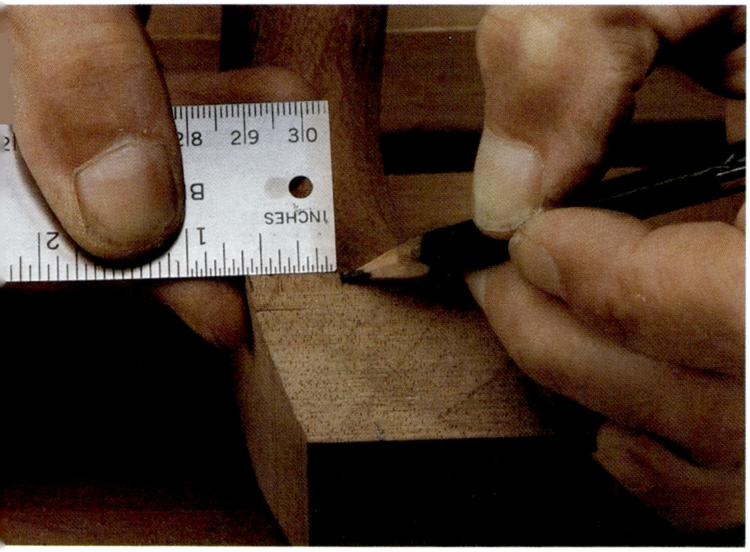

At the top edge of the foot measure in 5/8" from the back and make a mark.

Where the arc of the front toe touches the edge, make a mark on the side of the foot.

With a square draw a line from the point up the foot. Repeat all these markings on the other side.

Make a mark on the leg, 31/2" up from the bottom of the foot.

Make an arc across the top of the front toe, from mark to mark.

Carry this line around the leg. This is the stop at the top of the valleys between the toes.

Lay the pattern for the valley on the leg, aligning it with the upper line and the line of the back toe.

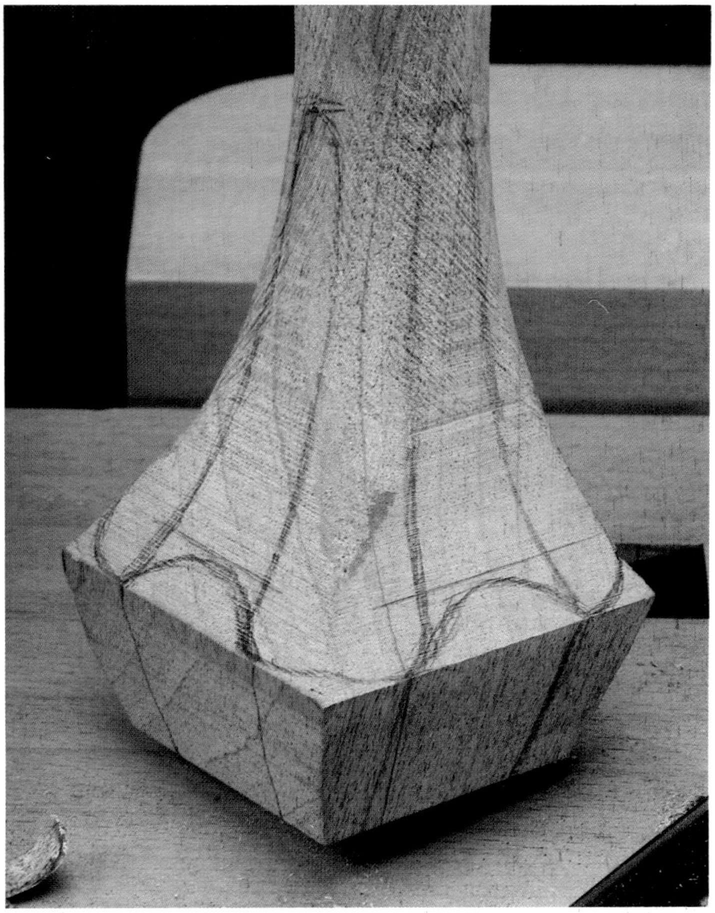

The toe layout is complete and we are ready to carve.

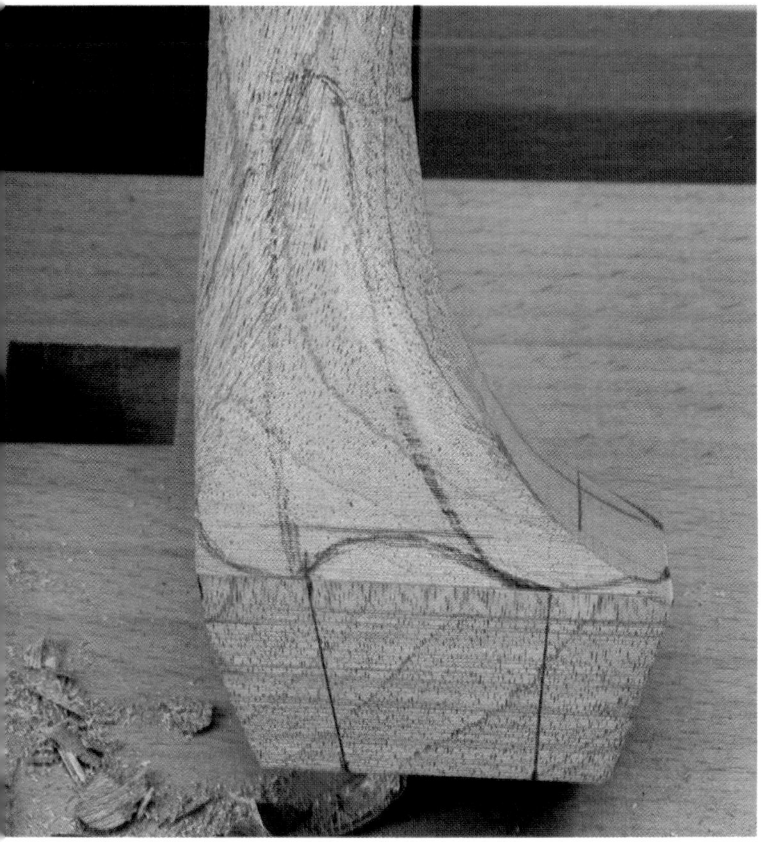

Draw the pattern. Flip the pattern and repeat on the other side.

Begin with the outside toe, rounding to the lines we have drawn. It will save sanding if you use a gouge that fits the curve. Otherwise a flat chisel will work just fine. Cut flat until you get to the line. If you start rounding too soon it is harder to keep a true shape.

Begin to round the toe over.

and the other side.

Bring the curve to the lines, top and bottom.

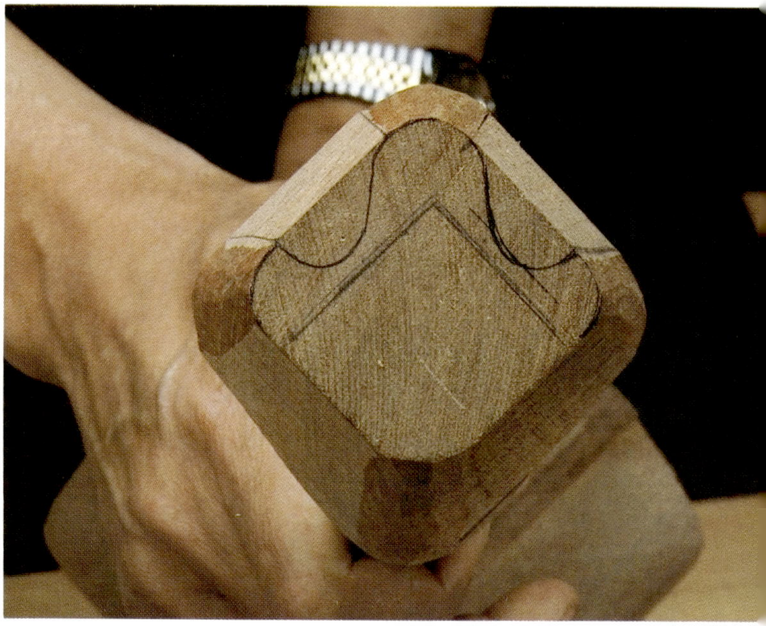

The toes roughed out as seen from the bottom ...

Follow the same steps for the middle toe...

and the top.

Next we move to the spaces between the toes. To remove material quickly we'll use a 9/13 gouge. Put it in the center of the space and apply pressure with a mallet, hitting it sharply.

Work your way from the to the bottom, going a little deeper with each pass.

Move to the side and cut away some more. Continue with this gouge until you've enlarged the trough. Don't go all the way to the lines.

The trough is roughly cut and ready for smoothing.

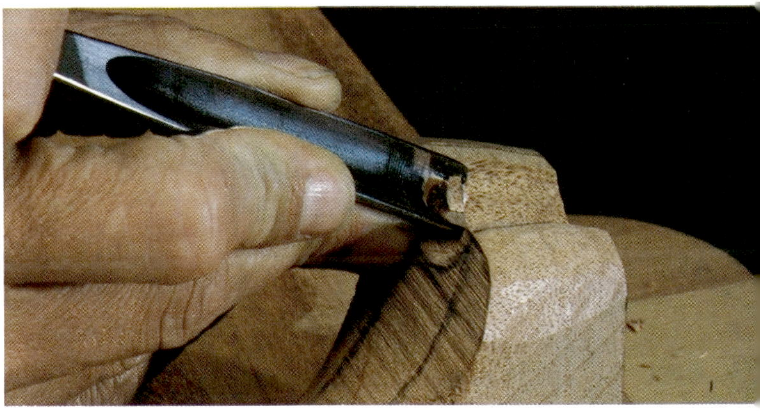

Switch to flatter gouge to clean up the trough. Go right to the lines with this tool, cleaning up the ridges left by the larger gouge.

With a flat chisel, round the middle toe into the trough.

Progress as seen from the bottom...

As you go up the leg, it should gradually blend in with the line of the leg.

and the top.

The rounded toe.

Use a flat chisel to round over the outside of the toe.

On the top of the foot use an 8/18 longbent or straight gouge to continue the space between the toe.

Use a series of short cuts to establish the profile of the trough.

With a smaller No. 8 gouge, begin working up the leg.

I have to stop here or the chips will tear in ways that I don't want.

This takes us to this point. The chisel kind of bottoms itself out creating a natural curve.

Come back from the top with a gouge that matches the radius of the top, a No.8/10.

Push the gouge in at the top of the trough.

Rotate it to one side...

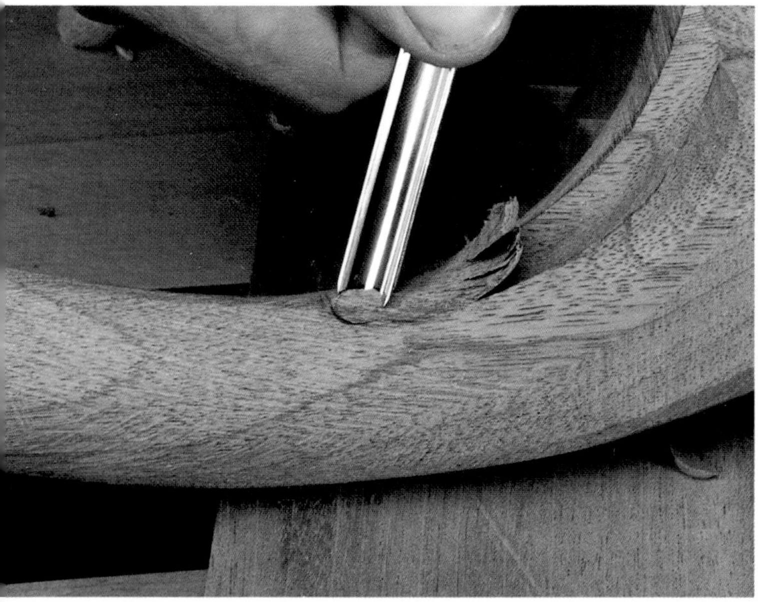

then the other.

Go back and continue the circle around.

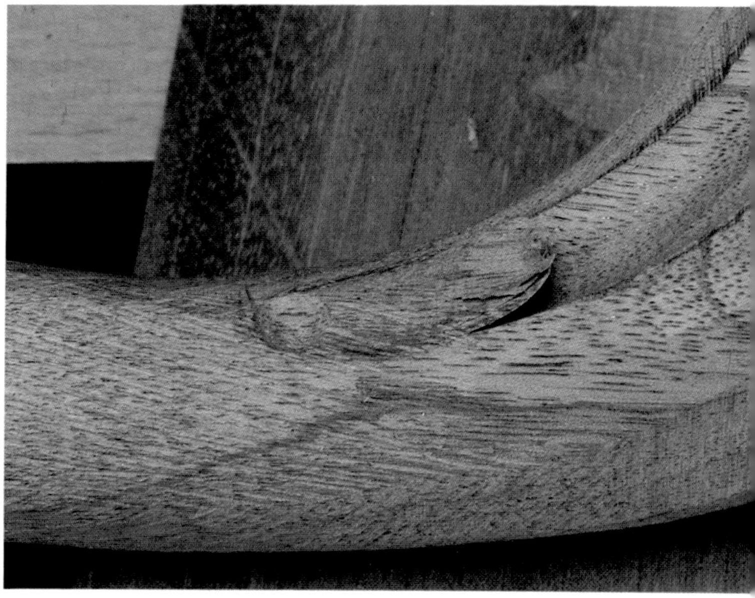

When the chip falls out it leaves a bowl shape. This spooning breaks the end grain and allows us to finish our upward cut.

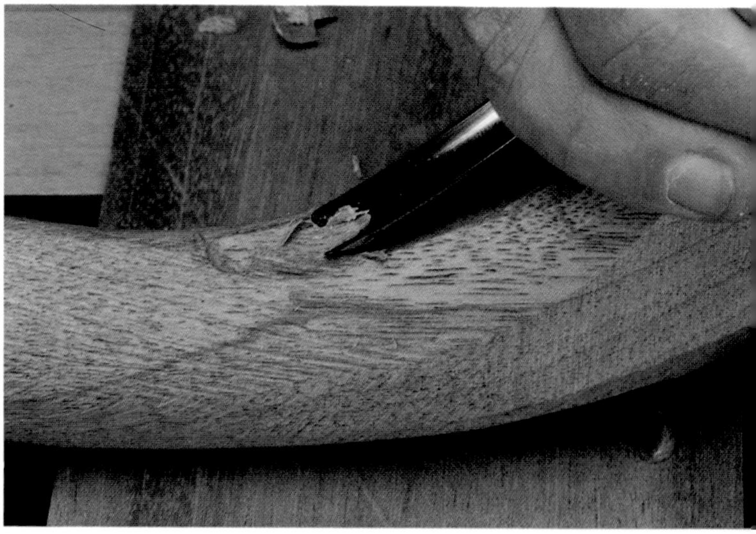

A bent gouge helps us to follow the curve of the cut. Run up into the bowl you've cut.

Now go back and clean up the trough.

Flatten the ridge left by the bandsaw on the top of the middle toe.

As you move up the toe you'll need to turn your chisel over so the beveled edge is down. Otherwise the curve of the leg will cause you to bite into it.

Round the front edge of the toe, doming at the middle of the toe.

Carry the curving up the toe, blending in at the ankle.

One half done.

Repeat the process on the other side.

The carved foot.

Put the rail in place, remembering to match the numbers. Use a scraper or chisel to make the post flush with the rail.

Fit the top of the knee return so it turns under the rail.

A router brings the molding around the corner of the post. This is done during a dry fitting, allowing you to make adjustments.

The finished corner

Finishing

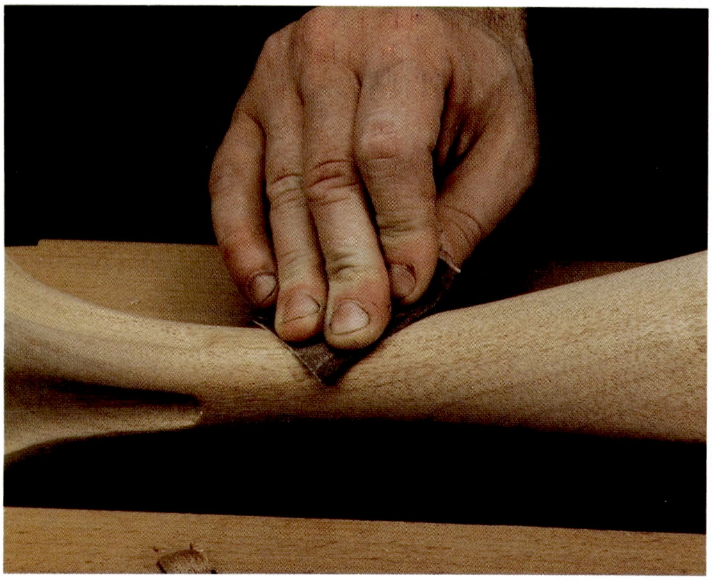

Disassemble the stool. Scrape to remove file and rasp marks. Progressively sand the legs and rails beginning with 100 grit paper, and working down to 180.

Lightly sand the carvings. The goal of sanding is to remove any machine markings and get a nice smooth finish.

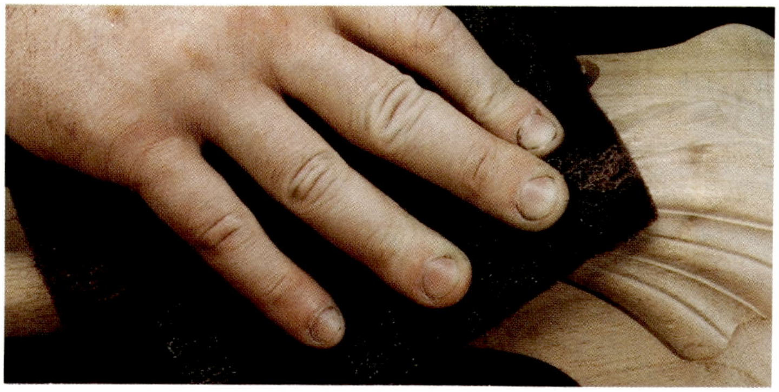

Lightly rub the whole piece with fine Scotchbrite™ pad to prepare it for staining.

The glue block in place and the inside of the post routed.

The slip seat frame should be made at this time. The corners can be mortised and tenoned or lap jointed, and it should be sized so there is 1/16" between the frame and the inside of the stool all around. Send it off to the upholsterer so it will be ready when you have completed the finishing process.

Glue the stool up and clamp it overnight. It is then ready for staining. Use brown mahogany water soluble aniline dye. It is a penetrating dye that gives good, clear colors, allowing the quality of the grain to show through. Apply it with a brush and get even coverage. One nice thing about the water based dye is that you can use a sponge to even the dye. A problem is that the dye raises the grain, so you might need to rub it down with Scotchbrite™ and apply a second coat.

Apply a coat of shellac. Shellac dries quickly so try not to work it too much.

Taking some of the surface water off with a paper towel helps it dry faster.

Follow instructions for drying times. When it dries, rub it down with 0000 steel wool.

Apply a second coat of shellac.

Apply a coat of brown or amber paste wax over the whole piece. Follow the directions on the can.

Rub the piece again with steel wool.

When it dries, buff it to a nice, pleasing shine.

Gallery

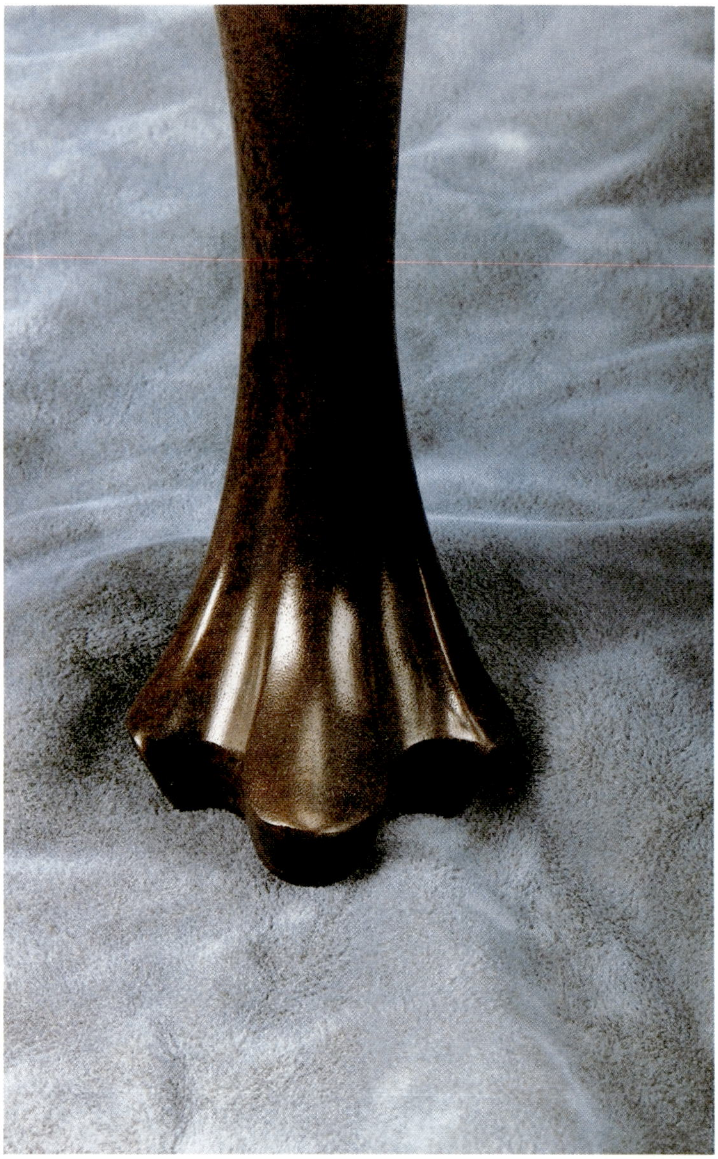